A FUTURE FOR OUR PAST?

An introduction to
heritage studies

Mark Brisbane ● John Wood

ENGLISH HERITAGE

CONTENTS

ABOUT THIS BOOK 3

WHAT IS HERITAGE? 4
Heritage, culture
and environment 4
A personal heritage 4
Heritage - the word 5

HERITAGE AS
INFORMATION 6
History and archaeology 6
Art and architecture 7
People and the environment 7

HERITAGE AS
PERCEPTION 8
Aesthetics and ambience 8
Association and symbolism 8
Whose heritage is it? 10

THREATS TO
THE HERITAGE 11
Acute threats 11
Chronic threats 11
Conceptual threats 13

CARING FOR
THE HERITAGE 14
Conservation -
a dynamic process 14
A redundant environment 15
New heritages 16
A European tradition? 16

HERITAGE
CONSERVATION 17
Identification 17
Survey and recording 17
Assessing the heritage 19
Environmental assessment 20
Setting priorities 21

PROTECTING
THE HERITAGE 22
Legal frameworks
and designation 22
Beneficial management 23
Management planning 24
Research 24
Education 25
Economic development 25

INTERPRETING
THE HERITAGE 27
Defining interpretation 27
Stages in interpretation 28
Why interpret? 29
Determining the audience 30
Designing interpretation 34
Types of presentation 35
Approaches to interpretation 35
Can it ever be unbiased? 39
Hot interpretation 40
Measuring effectiveness 40
Practical feedback 41

CONFLICTS IN
THE HERITAGE 42
Identifying and
resolving conflicts 42
Whose past is it anyway? 42
Current issues 44
Developing integrated
approaches 47

BIBLIOGRAPHY 50
Acknowledgements 52

English Heritage

2

ABOUT THIS BOOK

ABOVE LEFT: Stonehenge, Wiltshire. General view of the stones with Druid ceremony in progress, 22 June 1993.

ABOVE RIGHT:Windsor Castle. Archaeologists at work after the fire.

This book has been written primarily for use by staff and students in sixth forms, colleges of further and higher education and universities, where an increasing number of courses include heritage studies or related subjects. It will also appeal to anyone interested in our heritage and its conservation.

The heritage can arouse strong reactions: protests at the M3 construction at Twyford Down; police cordons at Stonehenge at the Summer Solstice; the public's shock as Windsor Castle is engulfed by fire and smoke.

Behind each of these images lies a complex set of issues. But what is heritage? How much of it should be protected, exploited or both? And what methods are appropriate to safeguard the heritage while making as much as possible accessible to the public?

This book examines these questions and aims to provide an introduction to the often complex and sometimes conflicting procedures which attempt to deal with the heritage, its conservation, management and interpretation. It concentrates on the physical heritage of historic buildings, landscapes and portable artefacts rather than the wider cultural heritage of folklore, literature, art, or music.

RIGHT: An anti-motorway protestor being carried off Twyford Down, Hampshire.

WHAT IS HERITAGE?

HERITAGE, CULTURE AND ENVIRONMENT

The heritage consists of those things of value that we have inherited and wish to keep for future generations. It is therefore important to establish what those things might be, why we want to keep them, and who 'we' are.

The heritage is also where culture meets the environment. It is concerned with things in the environment, whether constructed or natural, that are given cultural value and treated in special ways. It is therefore central to our understanding of our environment and our place within it.

However, defining the heritage in detail may be more difficult. If you ask people to define 'heritage' they may tell you about landscapes, music, theatre, literature, art, dance, clothing, food, language, architecture - all those things which give a culture its identity. As the first report of the National Heritage Memorial Fund put it in 1981,

"We could no more define the national heritage than we could define, say, beauty or art...So we decided to let the national heritage define itself. We awaited requests for assistance from those who believed they had a part of the national heritage worth saving..."

Despite this, the report then went on to present a definition of the national heritage, and an assessment of its possible value:

"The national heritage of this country is remarkably broad and rich. It is simultaneously a representation of the development of aesthetic expression and a testimony to the role played by the nation in world history.
The national heritage also includes the natural riches of Britain - the great scenic areas, the fauna and flora - which could so easily be lost by thoughtless development. Its potential for enjoyment must be maintained, its educational value for succeeding generations must be enriched and its economic value in attracting tourists to this country must be developed. But this national heritage is constantly under threat."

Looking at gravestones is a useful way of colecting data about our own, or our community's past.

So the value of the heritage, to the writers of the National Heritage Memorial Fund report, was to be seen as a matter of national pride, with potential for enjoyment, education and creating wealth. Its value is increased by its vulnerability.

However, this 'national' heritage is just one heritage among many. There are in the UK for example, a Welsh and a Scottish Gaelic heritage, a West Indian heritage, an aristocratic heritage, a railway heritage, a seafaring heritage, a nonconformist heritage, a culinary heritage, a heritage of the labour movement, a heritage of the women's movement. Each will be valued differently by different people. This makes decisions about conservation difficult - one group's valued feature may be another's irrelevance or eyesore. Heritages may even define themselves in opposition to each other, by exclusion rather than inclusion. 'Heritage' can mean racism and intolerance. It is a political minefield.

In this section a variety of aspects of the heritage are examined, but a sense of threat is common to all - that if something is not done, those who value this particular heritage will have lost something of value to them which cannot be replaced. It

Family photo albums are part of our individual heritage.

is not surprising that this sense is particularly prevalent today: we now have the means to destroy our culture and our environment at a rate which previous generations could hardly have imagined.

A PERSONAL HERITAGE

Everyone has a personal inheritance. For some people, there may be family heirlooms in the form of furniture, cutlery, or even houses or land. These have symbolic and associative values for the family to whom they belong, and are held in trust by each generation for the next.

Some people use documents, gravestones and datestones on buildings to trace their ancestral roots, in a search for information about individual identity.

For most of us, the heritage provides landmarks we can identify with, that give us a sense of belonging and a sense of our place in time and space. If a tree we knew as a child is cut down, or a familiar building in our neighbourhood is demolished, we feel a loss as if part of ourselves had gone. It is often only when something is threatened that we realise how much we value it.

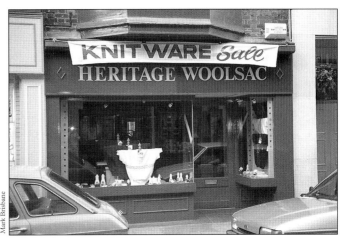

Trading on the value of the word and its associations, this so-called 'heritage' development is attempting to enhance its appeal.

Instant heritage products - a 'heritage' wool shop in Winchester.

HERITAGE - THE WORD

The word heritage comes from the French *heriter*, meaning to inherit. It formerly had specific legal meanings relating to wills and bequests, concerning family heirlooms and estates, and as a result it gained aristocratic connotations. Interestingly, and somewhat confusingly considering its French origins, the French, Portuguese and Italians tend to use a different word, namely *patrimony*, to indicate both the tangible and intangible inheritance from their cultural and personal past.

In the UK, the nineteenth century saw a development in the meaning and use of the word *heritage* to include the idea of a common inheritance belonging to a people or a country. 'Heritage' still conveys a sense of pride, of something we might wish to associate with - either individually or as a group. From the mid-1970s onwards, use of the term developed rapidly - as for example with 'European Architectural Heritage Year' in 1975.

Today, the word 'heritage' still seems to be increasing in currency. English Heritage adopted its popular name in 1984. In 1992, the government established a Department of National Heritage, and the government agency responsible for countryside and wildlife conservation in Scotland adopted the title Scottish Natural Heritage. Professor Peter Fowler claims to be one of the first to use the phrase 'the heritage industry' in 1985. (Fowler, 1992).

'Heritage' usually carries connotations of pride, tradition, identity, and quality. It is often associated with images of skilled craftsmanship and virtues of solidity, stability, longevity, and durability - desirable things which are now expensive, scarce, or no longer available. Advertisers are therefore finding that the word can be effective in selling almost anything from food to clothing and expensive cars. Unfortunately this means that, as with many other words, the meaning of the word 'heritage' is being destroyed and society may soon have to find an alternative word to replace it.

Because valued objects, sites, areas and landscapes may stand in the way of new developments, the heritage can provide a focus for opposition to change, and for those who dislike the modern world an opportunity for escapism or nostalgia. Such attitudes have, naturally enough, always been particularly strong at times of great social and economic change: the Gothic Revival and later the Arts and Crafts Movement in the nineteenth century were reactions to the impact of the Industrial Revolution.

More recently, tourist attractions have sprung up to cater for the growing demand for leisure activities, which have hoped to draw customers with images of the past. These 'heritage attractions' are often seen by local authorities as means of publicising some unique aspect of the locality and so attracting tourists.

As a result, for many people the word 'heritage' has unfortunately become identified with a particular type of tourist attraction - often of doubtful authenticity or quality. Heritage becomes associated with ideas of commercial exploitation, shallowness, and packaged history.

Robert Hewison attacked this aspect of heritage in 1987 in his book *The Heritage Industry: Britain in a climate of decline* which concludes,

"Instead of the miasma of nostalgia we need the fierce spirit of renewal; we must substitute a critical for a closed culture, we need history, not heritage. We must live in the future tense, and not the past pluperfect."

Hewison is wrong to identify heritage as nostalgia. Although it may be useful to the nostalgic, heritage is much more than this. In a world where established beliefs and social structures are increasingly challenged, an understanding of the past (however defined) provides a perspective on the present, a means to understand and make sense of it.

On the other hand, he is right to distinguish heritage from history. Although many people associate the word 'heritage' with history, they are different things. History is about the study of the past using evidence: landscapes, historic buildings and monuments, museum artefacts, documentary records, and oral traditions all provide evidence for the historian to use.

Although it consists of relics from the past, the heritage is not the past itself - the historian must interpret it to try and understand what happened and when. The heritage also has many other values apart from its usefulness as historical evidence.

HERITAGE AS INFORMATION

HISTORY AND ARCHAEOLOGY

The past has gone. Like the police investigating a crime, we can try to piece together the facts of what it was like or what happened by using witnesses or evidence. Witnesses can only take us back a short distance - as soon as we wish to go back before living memory we must use evidence.

Historians work mainly from archives consisting of records made in the past such as laws, financial accounts, property deeds, old maps, letters, diaries and other documents. All these are therefore valuable parts of the heritage. Historians need not be interested only in the great affairs of state. The history of religion, medicine, or literature for example are recognised studies in their own right.

Archaeologists primarily study the past directly through the actual rubbish and ruins (physical remains) rather than from written records. They compare different features and deposits, and analyse the relationships between them. Many people associate archaeology with prehistory - the period before written records were made. However, especially in the last fifty years, archaeologists have become interested in studying all periods of history, including the Industrial Revolution and beyond.

Archaeological researchers therefore may be interested not only in monuments such as Bronze Age barrows or hillforts, but also in medieval castles or deserted villages, buried deposits under urban centres, sites associated with industrial archaeology such as canals or windmills, and even field patterns in the countryside. These features, no less than the archives used by historians, have value as evidence of past activity.

Fountains Abbey, North Yorkshire. The ruins were incorporated into the landscaping scheme of the eighteenth century because of their romantic value.

In Tucson, Arizona, American archaeologists have been studying very recent remains indeed - the contents of peoples' dustbins! From these they have been able to discover a great deal about current social and economic activity in the locality which would not have been established from questioning people.

In general, archaeological research is interested in finding out either about people and societies and how they have related to each other (anthropological studies); or places and how they came to be as they are today (geographical studies); or the process of change through time (historical studies). Often, of course, more than one of these may be combined in a single project.

RIGHT: An urban excavation at Tower Street, Winchester.

ART AND ARCHITECTURE

Architectural and art historians use the physical heritage to study the development of designs and styles, including what these can tell us of the architects or artists who created them. Buildings, paintings, and sculptures are all therefore important parts of the heritage, valued for the evidence they can provide of past creativity and the contribution they have made to the development of modern aesthetic ideas.

England has made particular contributions to the development of the aesthetics of landscape. This can be studied in the places painted by Constable or Turner, and many of the places they painted are recognisable today. While their interest was in capturing the beauty of the existing landscape, eighteenth and nineteenth century landscape designers attempted to create attractive views by modifying the environment itself.

The history of landscape design is represented by surviving examples of parks and gardens, such as at Stourhead in Wiltshire or Castle Howard in Yorkshire: English Heritage, recognising their importance, has compiled an official register of these.

PEOPLE AND THE ENVIRONMENT

Historical ecologists are interested in the ways in which people have interacted with their surroundings in the past. Ancient woodlands, chalk and limestone grasslands, heaths and moors all represent long-established patterns of land management, which provide important evidence of ways in which people and the environment have interacted and influenced each other over many centuries.

Owing to their longevity, these areas have also become unique habitats, with some plants and animals dependent on them for their survival. Some have therefore been designated by English Nature and its sister organisations in other parts of the UK as *Sites of Special Scientific Interest* (SSI), to attempt to ensure that they survive for future generations. Such areas form an important part of the heritage.

Apart from these constructed habitats, many other aspects of the heritage may have significance for

communities of plants and animals. Ancient stone walls and buildings can provide homes for plant species that have become rare elsewhere; old quarries can become important nature reserves as the natural process of plant colonisation takes place; old roofs provide homes for bats, swallows and housemartins; ponds and water channels are colonised by newts and dragonflies.

Sometimes, these ecological values may conflict with archaeological values, as where, for example, badgers (a protected species) take up residence in a prehistoric burial mound. Elsewhere they may complement one another: environmental archaeologists for example study past environments through the remains of wood, seeds, pollen, molluscs and bones. Wetlands in particular can be important in providing anaerobic conditions in which organic material survives.

As our knowledge of our environment and its past grows, so will our understanding of what constitutes heritage. This is because, as research techniques improve, we see potential for information in features or artefacts we had previously overlooked.

BELOW: Chysauster, Cornwall. A prehistoric settlement in an area of botanical importance, recently designated a Site of Special Scientific Interest.

A Bronze Age trackway, Becton, East London. These fragile archaeological remains survived in peat deposits found in the former marshlands of the River Thames. Although increasingly at risk, these wetland conditions do occur notably in the Somerset Levels (see page 22).

Canford Heath, Dorset has been maintained by a particular type of land management system for centuries. As traditional management declines, so does the characteristic feature dependent upon it, unless it can be artificially maintained by grants or legislation. In addition, some landscapes are particularly vulnerable to change and encroachment: the decline in area of the heathland in Dorset has been dramatic, from 30,000 hectares in 1820 to under 5,000 hectares in 1980.

HERITAGE AS PERCEPTION

AESTHETICS AND AMBIENCE

Apart from its value as evidence of past activity, the heritage has a much wider power to inspire and move people. Landscapes, paintings, buildings or small artefacts can be visually attractive. Ever since the Romantic Movement of the late eighteenth and early nineteenth centuries, monastic ruins, hills, and lakes have carried an aesthetic appeal which continues to provide a powerful impulse for conservation.

Rugged coasts have been designated *Heritage Coasts* by the Countryside Commission. Upland areas such as the Peak District in Derbyshire or Dartmoor in Devon have become National Parks. In the USA, the national parks movement went further, and large areas were set aside as permanent wilderness. Yosemite Valley in California, one of the first of these, is noted for its dramatic rock formations.

Even where a place is not immediately visually appealing, a sense of mortality or of one's place in the long continuum of time can be conveyed by an ambience or historic atmosphere. Thus the ruins of a monastery or the remains of an old industrial site can be enjoyed by many people who know little about archaeology.

Tintern Abbey, Gwent. In 1770 William Gilpin proposed taking a mallet to the ruins of Tintern Abbey to improve its silhouette.

ASSOCIATION AND SYMBOLISM

The Lake District is an attractive place to visit in its own right, but its appeal is enhanced by the area's association with Wordsworth, Coleridge and the other Lake Poets in the early nineteenth century. Visitors come to experience the area these poets were describing, and to understand and appreciate better the poets and the poetry itself. Other places with powerful associative value include Dedham Vale in Suffolk for its association

BELOW: Whitby Abbey, North Yorkshire. Whitby has many associations with charismatic individuals, some real, such as Captain Cook, others less so, such as Count Dracula.

A Blue Plaque erected by English Heritage.

with the painter, John Constable, or Thomas Hardy's Dorset.

An area with limited aesthetic appeal can still have associative value: battlefields may have no upstanding features but still be evocative; blue plaques on otherwise dull London houses record famous former residents.

In other places, associative values can also be artificially inflated: visitors to South Tyneside, Catherine Cookson Country, will see very little that they could recognise from her books. Instead, the title is used by the District Council as a way of attracting visitors who can then be shown a variety of other attractions unrelated to Catherine Cookson such as the South Shields Roman Fort or the Bede Monastery Museum. The policy has led to disappointment for some Catherine Cookson devotees, and also for some other visitors who would rather identify the region with the Romans or the Venerable Bede than the characters and places of Catherine Cookson's books. Nevertheless it has apparently been successful in attracting tourists to an area they might not otherwise have visited.

It is interesting to note that places which feature in TV series, like 'Last of the Summer Wine', are now developing an associative value of their own, with visitors keen to see them for themselves. Presumably such places will retain their associative value only as long as the TV series is remembered.

Association with cultural events, people or institutions can give the heritage powerful symbolic value. Symbols help the individual identify with or against a group, an idea, or a place. They can therefore be socially integrative or divisive, and cannot be ideologically or politically neutral. The Coronation Chair is a symbol of the English Monarchy, just as the Stone of Scone is a symbol of the Scottish one. The chair is, of course, just a chair, the stone just a stone, but their symbolic importance is enormous.

The Houses of Parliament, and Big Ben in particular, have become symbols of British national identity. The American Statue of Liberty and Liberty Bell in Pennsylvania are US equivalents. Religious sites and monuments have powerful symbolism of their own: Jerusalem is important to Jews, Christians and Muslims alike; Bodh Gaya in

northern India, where the Buddha attained enlightenment, has attracted temples from several Buddhist countries.

The heritage is often seen as providing a collective relationship with an accepted, authorised past. This may be by individual choice, as part of a conscious desire to belong to a group. Some past events may be emphasised and given symbolic value - as for example in Northern Ireland where the (Protestant) king William of Orange defeated (Catholic) James II at the Battle of the Boyne in 1690 is commemorated by the Ulster Unionists every 12th July - and any material remains of this battle (such as weapons, standards and so on) have acquired an enhanced value to the Unionist community.

ABOVE: The Houses of Parliament and Big Ben are symbols of both national identity and the democratic process.

Belfast, Northern Ireland: In recent times both Protestant and Catholic groups have demonstrated their allegiances on walls inside their own communities.

Statue of Boadicea, opposite the Houses of Parliament, London. Boudica, her correct name, was the Celtic queen of the Iceni tribe who led a revolt against the Roman occupation of Britain in AD 60. The statue was cast in the early 1900s as Britain's first national heroine.

Because the heritage has power to stir the emotions and reinforce group identities, it cannot exist in an ideological or political vacuum. Politicians and others will often seek to promote a view of the heritage that supports or justifies their views or policies. George Orwell's book *1984* included a 'Ministry of Truth' which continually rewrote history to demonstrate that the ruling party had always been right. Nazi Germany harnessed archaeology to support its theory of a master race. The political misuse of heritage serves to underline its importance as evidence.

The removal of a political or ideological power can result in the removal of its symbols too: with the collapse of communism, thousands of statues of Stalin and Lenin were removed from towns and cities in Eastern Europe and the former Soviet Union. People preferred not to commemorate them.

WHOSE HERITAGE IS IT?

In a sense, all heritage is common to all humanity. The United Nations, through UNESCO, has tried to emphasise this through the 1972 World Heritage Convention which establishes a list of World Heritage Sites of international importance.

Society consists of a great variety of groups and interests who may have different - and sometimes conflicting - interests. These groups may be defined economi-cally, geographically, by age, by occupation, by religion, or by ethnic or national group. Different groups may identify with, or against, different aspects of the heritage, or ascribe different values to the same place.

Stonehenge is valued by many different groups for different reasons. The 'Druids' regard it as their temple. Astronomers claim it as a prehistoric observatory designed on celestial alignments. To some 'New Age' travellers it is an 'earth mystery'; to others it has become a symbol of state oppression. Architects and engineers appreciate its sophisticated design. For archaeologists it is evidence of a particular Bronze Age culture and part of a prehistoric landscape. To many tourists it is simply a famous place they have heard of and are curious to see for themselves.

ABOVE: Stonehenge, Wiltshire.

RIGHT: A demonstrator pounds away at the Berlin Wall as East German border guards look on from above at the Brandenburg Gate, 11 November 1989. Should some part of the Wall have been preserved to remind us of the divisions it once symbolised?

THREATS TO THE HERITAGE

Heritage develops extra values in an age of change. This section examines threats to the heritage and ways in which the heritage is looked after.

Threats to the heritage may be divided into two main categories: *acute* (those which are likely to be immediate and devastating); and *chronic* (those which will lead to gradual attrition if not checked). Both types may be natural or caused by people.

ACUTE THREATS

Acute threats of a natural kind include earthquakes, volcanic eruptions (like that which devastated Pompeii and Herculaneum in the first century AD), landslides, or sudden, violent storms (including lightning).

The most devastating acute threats are from war damage. This can result either from deliberate attempts to demoralise the enemy, as with the bombing of Dresden or Coventry in the Second World War, or incidental, as where a heritage site happens to have strategic importance by being situated at a river crossing, a port, or close to a military installation. British newspapers reported during the war which followed Iraq's invasion of Kuwait that Iraqi weapons were being deliberately stored in World Heritage Sites where no doubt they were considered safe from UN attack. In the Bosnian conflict, 'ethnic cleansing' has extended to the demolition of religious and cultural buildings associated with rival factions.

Many other acute threats also exist, of course. The authorities may decide, for example, to sacrifice heritage sites or areas for some purpose deemed to be more important. During the Second World War the Ministry of Defence requisitioned Tyneham, Dorset and Imber, Wiltshire for military training. More recently, planning decisions by national or local authorities on new developments or civil engineering projects have constituted acute threats - as with the M3 Winchester bypass. The devastating fires at Uppark House, Sussex (see page 38), Windsor Castle, and Hampton Court Palace appear to have arisen from human error.

An acute threat demands an immediate and drastic response - usually an attempt to salvage whatever information can be retrieved about the site or feature before it is destroyed.

Wherever possible, heritage conservation attempts to avoid acute threats by ensuring that all alternatives are properly explored before decisions are made. This is where procedures such as environmental assessment can be of use.

CHRONIC THREATS

Chronic threats, leading to the gradual destruction of the heritage, may also be natural or the result of human activity. Natural threats can include weather patterns over a number of years, or coastal erosion. In the latter case, direct conflict between conservation interests is possible: Hurst Castle in Hampshire, for example, is a Scheduled Monument, being washed away by the sea. The coast on which it stands is designated a Site of Special Scientific Interest for its coastal erosion processes.

ABOVE: The Rose Theatre, London, under excavation. The site was the location of one of the theatres in which the plays of William Shakespeare and other Elizabethan playwrights were first performed. Its discovery and the subsequent publicity caused a major conflict between the preservation of the archaeological remains and the development of the site.

Tyneham, Dorset. The Ministry of Defence requisitioned the village during the Second World War for training purposes, but has never returned it to its previous inhabitants. Today most of the houses are conserved as ruins and the public is occasionally admitted to see the site.

Hurst Castle, Hampshire, where the processes of coastal erosion have produced a conflict of interest between the needs of an historic site and an SSSI.

Chronic human threats can include long term policies for development or change, or land management strategies which are inimical to the continued survival of valued features.

These could include

■ ongoing destructive management, such as ploughing on earthworks, which will gradually reduce them to nothing

■ development plans or estate management plans which ignore heritage conservation interests

■ designs for roads, pipelines or other civil engineering projects which destroy valued landscapes, habitats and archaeological sites

■ incautious or ill-informed promotion of tourism development which can destroy the very features that tourists have come to see

■ pollution, such as acid rain, which destroys stone monuments, for example castles and abbeys

■ economic changes that affect how a particular part of the heritage is maintained (Between 1918 and 1945, for example 485 country houses were demolished when families could no longer afford them)

With chronic threats, a more considered response is usually possible, and an opportunity may be afforded for public debate about relative priorities. However if not attended to, chronic threats will become acute. Neglect is perhaps the most dangerous chronic threat - emphasising the need for active management.

One form of chronic threat often overlooked is that of adaptive re-use. Our culture and environment are constantly being adapted to new perceptions and needs. Old farmworkers' cottages, for example, must be fitted with bathrooms and modern kitchens if they are to continue in use as houses.

Preserved, protected sites and monuments must also be actively consolidated and maintained in a

English Heritage

safe condition if they are to be visited by the public. Great houses and gardens designed to be cared for by armies of staff must be adapted to maintenance by few people using modern equipment. Authenticity is lost, but the process is unavoidable. We will return to this later.

Woodhouse Mill, Todmorden, West Yorkshire. A derelict mill faces an uncertain future. What changes of use are acceptable as well as economically viable?

University of Cambridge

An aerial view of a deserted medieval village at Braybrooke, Northamptonshire. Modern farming techniques can quickly obliterate sites unless thay are protected like this one.

CONCEPTUAL THREATS

As we have seen, different groups apply different values to their and others' heritage. Some of these differences may result in what may be termed conceptual threats. The heritage conserver needs to be aware of these, and must also attempt to define balanced priorities which respect a variety of interests without regarding all views as equally valid. This means justifying decisions taken, recognising bias and prejudice, and wherever possible encouraging open-minded debate. It also means being prepared to challenge orthodoxies and change one's views if the evidence supports this. It is undoubtedly the most challenging aspect of heritage conservation, to which there is no 'right' answer.

Apart from heritages which identify themselves against each other, there are many common attitudes which can threaten heritage conservation as a whole. Often, such attitudes are in fact partial, and apply only to the heritage you don't value. Some examples of such attitudes are given below. In each case, the attitude is followed by the possible consequence for the heritage. It can be an interesting exercise to conduct a poll of attitudes to the heritage in general, or to specific sites or areas, to see how prevalent these are and perhaps add others:

■ 'heritage is bunk' (rejection)

■ 'heritage is whatever you make it' (manipulation)

■ 'heritage is not interesting' (neglect)

■ 'heritage is a mystery' (ignorance? - some people prefer their heritage this way)

In practice, the conservation of the heritage cannot always be given the highest priority: local councillors may decide to allow the construction of a job-providing business park on an ancient meadow, for example. Aesthetic considerations may demand the removal of an unsightly disused industrial site despite its great information and associative value for local people. Increased leisure time may demand the construction of a golf course on a deserted village site. Politics may

demand that only 'acceptable' or 'marketable' aspects of the heritage are funded.

However the case both for and against the conservation of a valued part of the heritage should at least be aired. Often, damage may be avoidable if a development can be sited or a road routed to avoid an ancient monument or valued ancient woodland. This principle of sustainable development - balancing the needs of both new and old - is at the heart of heritage conservation.

Hampshire Chronicle

ABOVE: **Twyford Down, Hampshire, in 1993, the scene of the M3 Winchester bypass protests over the destruction of the Down.**

BELOW: **Waxham barn, Norfolk. A sadly neglected thirteenth-century barn.**

English Heritage

CARING FOR THE HERITAGE

As we have seen, the heritage is a powerful force in everyone's life, with important informational and perceptual values. However, as there is no complete agreement on what should constitute this heritage, and different things and places may be differently valued by different people, heritage conservation is no easy task.

The motivation to conserve the heritage arises from the values we have discussed that the individual or the group places on it. Curiosity about the world, past and present, and a desire to understand it; anxiety that familiar and cherished places (and therefore perceptions based on these) may be destroyed; and an aesthetic sense that sees beauty in the old and long-established all have a part to play. Heritage conservation must therefore attempt several very difficult things:

■ to understand the different types of heritage, the values placed upon them, and the ways in which they interconnect;

■ to balance the demands of present interest groups and individuals in reaching justified and documented decisions on how to manage the heritage so it survives, wherever possible, for future generations;

■ to resist political and commercial pressures to distort or deny aspects of the heritage, and respect the needs and views of minority groups and interests;

■ to be open to changing values and ideas and avoid dogma;

■ to ensure that we have not prevented future generations from valuing and benefiting from as yet unidentifiable interests and demands. We must therefore document our decisions so they at least know why we selected the things we did to pass on to them.

English Heritage

Bury St Edmunds, Suffolk. After the Dissolution the abbey was stripped of valuable building material apart from the abbot's house. Some of the ruins were converted into houses in the nineteenth century.

The heritage is by definition valuable and vulnerable. If examined critically, it is a means to understanding ourselves, our environment, and our past. Its conservation is therefore not about promoting a particular set of cultural values, but about encouraging a critical debate on the past, present, and possible future of those things of value that we - as individuals and as a group - have inherited.

CONSERVATION - A DYNAMIC PROCESS

Many people think of the heritage as a fossilisation of the past. In reality, the past has, by definition, gone. All we have are surviving fragments of its creations. Conservation therefore cannot be about static preservation but dynamic management and research. Left to itself, the cultural heritage, in all its forms - as well as much of the natural heritage - would gradually disappear through natural decay, and without study it would become meaningless.

Our environment has been shaped by the interaction of people with nature over many thousands of years, creating landscapes, buildings and artefacts that collectively bear witness to the process. Tastes and ideas change from generation to generation, and these changes are reflected in the physical environment we live in.

Physical, conceptual, and aesthetic structures are created and used in a cycle of cultural and environmental change which reflects the natural cycle of life and death. After a time structures are either destroyed to make way for new ones, or develop heritage values which help them survive.

If they survive it is inevitable that they will be adapted to new situations and requirements. In the case of physical, material heritage this means that original features are lost which could have provided important evidence of the people who built them and the environmental, social, conceptual and economic context in which they did so. Few people today, for example, would wish to live and work in a completely unmodified medieval building, lacking modern sanitation or other comforts. Static preservation is therefore impossible. Even the 'preservation' of a monument for its heritage values is an adaptation from its original purpose.

New features are written over the old, creating a palimpsest. Originally the word palimpsest meant a medieval legal document, written on parchment, which had been used more than once. Often it was possible to read earlier documents which had not been completely erased when the parchment was re-used.

Sometimes such documents could be recycled many times. In fact, our landscapes, our old buildings and even our cultures themselves are like this. Fragments of old features and ideas are often still visible beneath the surface of the modern world if we look for them.

Since culture is constantly developing and dynamic, and since the natural world too constantly decays and renews itself, it is impossible ever to preserve the past itself - or even the present - for the future. All we can do is identify those cultural landmarks that help us understand ourselves, our past, and our environment; make ourselves aware of changing cultural values; and examine the implications such changes might have on the things we value.

We have already examined some of the values given to the heritage. Underlying them is the need to make sense of the world - we like to feel that the world we left when we went to sleep is the same one we find when we wake in the morning. We also transmit our understanding of the world and of ourselves to the next generation through our culture. Letters, words, images, writing, myths, and the landmarks in our environment are all essential to this transmission.

Until the Industrial Revolution, environmental and cultural changes were usually slow enough to allow people to adapt to them. This was not always true - the dissolution of the monasteries in the mid-sixteenth century, for example, represented a revolutionary change in both culture and environment. Such times produced unrest - and an increased interest in the things that had been destroyed.

Conservation cannot stop the cycle. Repairs must be carried out, historic buildings must be kept weatherproof, the needs of visitors must be accommodated if a site is to be appreciated and understood by the public. All these necessary activities involve changes. Sometimes the value of a site, building, or landscape lies in the evidence provided for this very process of adaptation and change in the past. The removal of the accretions of later centuries by British archaeologists in the early nineteenth century revealed the original form or plan of the Parthenon in Athens, but it robbed us of the possibility of understanding how the building was used and appreciated by medieval people.

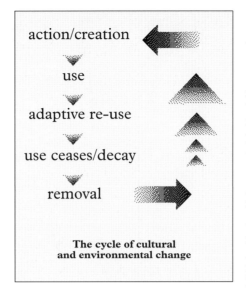

The cycle of cultural and environmental change

A REDUNDANT ENVIRONMENT

Today, with modern technology, virtually all of the traditional activities which maintained the character and value of the heritage are in rapid decline, while it has also become possible to modify or destroy our surroundings on a previously unimaginable scale. This situation brings with it a new sense of responsibility - a need to make careful and justifiable decisions on how to shape the future.

Sometimes the environment is deliberately modified to reflect a perceived demand. When a new road is built to relieve traffic pressure on existing ones, a specific and conscious decision has to be taken that the need for the road outweighs the cultural or environmental values destroyed by its construction.

New life was given to this eighteenth-century silk mill in Streatham, London when a supermarket adapted it to a new use.

English Heritage

In other cases, environmental changes are (as they have always been) unintentional by-products of changing values in society. Now, as society changes more quickly in response to changing technology, the environment changes too. The internal combustion engine and the jet aircraft have produced the most dramatic changes of all.

In the countryside, the mechanisation of farming means fewer people are needed to work the land, or to provide services for those who do, so the traditional role of the rural community has gone. Mechanised farming has little use for traditional farm buildings, small hedged fields, old meadows or unimproved grassland. Village blacksmiths, once common, have all but disappeared. Local mills no longer operate.

As former agricultural workers look for alternative work in towns, their village houses may be bought and adapted by urban professional people who wish to live in the country. As more people shop at large supermarkets on the urban fringe, so village shops, post-offices and public houses disappear. Many village inhabitants commute to the town by car, requiring more and wider roads to accommodate them. Increasing car ownership means fewer bus services for those without them.

Other 'incomers' move to the country on retirement, or acquire holiday homes for occasional residence only, so have no children to send to the local school. Small village schools are closed and children are transported by car to fewer, larger ones. Sometimes incomers object to slow farm machinery on the roads, or to rural sounds or smells that do not match their idealised view of what the country should be like. The village becomes suburbia; the character of the farmed countryside is maintained only by artificial subsidies to farmers.

In the towns, increasing car ownership and changing lifestyles mean that traditional small shops in town centres close, or are taken over by large companies who impose their corporate style on the high street. Living accommodation above the shops lies empty and deteriorating as shop managers now live in the suburbs, or in surrounding villages. Urban as well as rural customers with cars increasingly shop at the large stores on the urban fringe, which offer ample free car parking for their customers. Many of them work on large industrial or office parks on the edge of town. In the evenings, only the young pub and club-goers venture into the town centre, which is otherwise deserted. Its traditional role as a centre of economic and social activity for all groups and ages has gone.

Churches face increasing redundancy with the decline in churchgoing; town-halls are no longer needed for abolished local councils; changes in the health service and policies of 'care in the community' mean that long-established hospitals close.

In these circumstances, either we deliberately conserve at least a sample of those things that give our country, region or locality its character, or we must accept that all will be rapidly swept away.

Heritage conservation is no longer only about the exceptional site, building, or area. Owing to technological advance, we must now debate what future we want for every aspect of our environment, world-wide.

The heritage is part of both the culture and the environment; and since these are constantly changing in response to the demands of each generation and new technology, static preservation is not always possible or desirable. While a feature continues in its original use few will pause to notice it. However once it becomes obsolete, and pressure mounts to adapt it or replace it, its potential as evidence for past (or passing) ways of life becomes apparent, and its familiarity as part of the local scene is no longer taken for granted. The Royal Commission on the Historical Monuments of England has recently begun a survey of redundant collieries before they are demolished.

NEW HERITAGES

Objects, buildings, and landscapes are created, used, modified to new uses, and destroyed all the time. New features are therefore continually being created which may become the valued heritage of the next generation. Familiar features even of recent origin in our surroundings take on a special value at a time of great technical and social change - especially when the future of the world seems uncertain, with the media carrying stories of potential environmental disaster - as they help to give meaning and orientation to the world and ourselves. In these circumstances, it is not surprising that examples of post-war architecture are already being listed as having special importance, that archaeologists are now taking an interest in Second World War defences, and that museums are collecting examples of cars, cookers and computers.

A EUROPEAN TRADITION?

Heritage conservation is by no means confined to Europe, but has a long tradition in Asia and other parts of the world. Nevertheless, the importance of the material heritage in particular has been strengthened by the western, scientific tradition with its roots in the eighteenth-century Enlightenment, the European Renaissance of the fifteenth and sixteenth centuries, and ultimately in the philosophy of Aristotle. The scientific culture proposes that there is an objective world which can be understood by objective testing of hypotheses against evidence.

Because nothing is sacred and everything is challenged, this culture leads to uncertainty as cherished beliefs and structures are demolished by scientific advance. This must be set against the traditional post-Enlightenment belief in progress, which sustains much scientific work.

Conversely every aspect of our environment can constitute evidence for something if we wish it to. Ironically, therefore, while science challenges assumptions and promotes a belief in progress, it must also protect its data source. This can lead to the notion that everything is so important that nothing should be destroyed - a strictly preservationist approach, in which everything is sacred!

In contrast, the traditional Japanese approach to conservation is more concerned with the spirit of a place (*genius loci*) rather than its material fabric. Temples have been taken down and replaced using identical methods and materials at regular intervals over more than 1000 years. Each temple represents a tradition, and has symbolic and religious value, but at any one time the structure is usually no more than twenty five years old.

Royal Commission on Historical Monuments

HERITAGE CONSERVATION

IDENTIFICATION

The process of conservation starts with identification. Buildings, archaeological features, landscapes and other aspects of the heritage must be identified as having value that is worth conserving. At present, it is often the case that archaeologists, architects, ecologists, tourist bodies and other interests will make their own identifications - and problems of co-ordination can result.

Even within individual disciplines, there are often special interests that may contend. In archaeology, for example, the priorities of the prehistorian may not coincide with those of the post-medieval industrial archaeologist. Even where specialists and experts agree, the wider public through its elected local or national representatives may not. Thus even at this preliminary stage the process requires a degree of consensus.

For this reason alone, there is a need to develop, through education and training programmes, increased debate between different interest groups, and skills in balancing different interests and views. Heritage conservation is emerging as a demanding academic study in its own right.

SURVEY AND RECORDING

Survey is essential for heritage conservation. It takes two principal forms: prospection for new sites and features, and data collection about known ones. In either case this usually means a survey in the field but may include documentary and map searches.

In many cases, survey can be a straightforward task which does not require expensive equipment. In fact there are many schools and amateur groups now carrying out surveys of habitats, archaeological sites and historic buildings. Industrial and military sites in particular are often poorly documented and a simple measured survey may provide the only record - even of structures of quite recent origin, like Second World War pillboxes. Such data should be collated and made available for research and management purposes. This need not necessarily mean publication in the traditional sense: all over the UK there are heritage records and databases which generally welcome new information and make it available to the public.

Ecological and archaeological records

People have been systematically collecting information on plant, animal and bird communities for over 200 years, and much of this is available from County Wildlife Trusts or local museums. English Nature, the Countryside Council for Wales, and Scottish Natural Heritage all maintain records of areas of special ecological value such as Sites of Special Scientific Interest (SSSIs).

The collected data is used to assess the value of an archaeological site or area and for management purposes. This requirement needs to be borne in mind during the survey. Any management information which can be gleaned - how the site has been treated in the past, or is being treated now, and the effects of the treatment - needs to be carefully retained.

At present there is a need for more detailed information about the effect on buried archaeological sites of particular types of land management, including grazing grassland, ploughing, burrowing animals and tree-root action, and of different types of building foundation design. This is gradually being remedied: for example in Orkney, Historic Scotland have been examining the effects of rabbit damage on burial mounds. In an urban context, English Heritage are now commissioning Urban Deposit Surveys for historic centres such as London, York and Cirencester. In York, the civil engineers Ove Arup and Partners, together with York City Council, York University's Archaeology Department and English Heritage have used the deposit survey to develop new approaches to design-

The National Monuments Record Centre, Swindon. The NMR is part of the Royal Commission on Historical Monuments for England. The centre is housed in the refurbished General Offices of the Great Western Rasilway, and includes spacious search rooms for public use and a new wing (on the right of this picture), containing one of the finest archive facilities in Europe.

Royal Commission on Historical Monuments

ing foundations for buildings to minimise damage to buried archaeology. This exercise has stimulated a lively debate, including the issue of whether or not there is an acceptable loss of important archaeological urban deposits due to re-development (a maximum figure of 5% is suggested in the Ove Arup study for York).

Many different heritage features are subject to coastal erosion and those on the sea bed like sunken wrecks are vulnerable to changing currents, damage from fishing gear, looting by divers, microbial damage, etc. Recording of underwater and intertidal sites, and research into various destructive processes are still in their infancy, but the Archaeological Diving Unit based at the University of St.Andrews, and the RCHM in England have begun to approach the problem. Some local authorities, such as the Isle of Wight and Highland Region, Scotland, have begun to develop maritime sites and monuments records.

Archaeological sites

For archaeological sites, each English county and some districts have a database known as a *Sites and Monuments Record* (SMR), maintained by the local authority. In Wales, some SMRs are held by archeological trusts that cover more than one county. In Scotland, SMRs cover most (pre-1996) regional and island areas,whilst in London the record is held by English Heritage. Many (but not all) of these SMRs hold information about historic buildings, and some local authorities are combining them with ecological and countryside data to form integrated databases. Current local government reorganisation in all three countries will require a greater variety of approaches from one locality to another.

England, Scotland, and Wales also each have a Royal Commission on ancient or historical monuments which maintains a central *National Monuments Record* (NMR). This includes information on buildings and archaeological sites. Organisations such as the National Trust and some National Park authorities maintain their own records. In Northern Ireland , the Department of Environment (Northern Ireland) maintains a sites and monuments record in

Ferriby on the River Humber. The remains of Bronze Age boats, the oldest planked boats found in Northern Europe, were discovered in 1937 and excavated in the 1960s (see Bibliography page 52).

Belfast. In the Isle of Man the SMR is held by the Manx Museum, while the Channel Islands have their own heritage trusts.

If an archaeological site is to be unavoidably destroyed it may be recorded beforehand. This means the destruction of the site by excavation or dismantling and the creation of as accurate a record as possible of what was there.

In November 1990, the Government through the Department of the Environment issued its *Planning Policy Guidance 16* (PPG16) for England on archaeology and planning. Similar guidance to planning authorities has been subsequently issued in Wales (PPG16 Wales) and Scotland (NPPG5). These set out clearly how archaeology should be dealt with in the planning process. The first preference is for preservation in-situ, by designing developments in such a way as to minimise their impact on the archaeological resource. Where damage is unavoidable, it is the developer's responsibility to ensure that a proper record is made of those features that will be destroyed. This is normally prepared to a brief supplied by the developer's archaeological consultant or the planning authority's archaeological adviser to ensure that professional standards are met through the application of the most effective techniques and the documentation of aims, objectives and methodologies.

The guidance has marked a significant shift in perception of 'rescue' archaeology in Britain. Previously development was largely seen as providing an opportunity for archaeologists to do research. Now the emphasis is on retaining as far as possible a documented, retrievable resource which future researchers can use if required.

Historic buildings

In September 1994, the Department of the Environment issued *Planning Policy Guidance 15* (PPG15) for England entitled 'Planning and the Historic Environment'. This provides a full statement of Government policies for the identification and protection of historic buildings, conservation areas, and other elements of the historic environment such as historic battlefields and World Heritage Sites. It explains the role played by the planning system in protecting these sites and complements the guidance on archaeology and planning mentioned above (PPG16).

In addition PPG15 provides guidance to planning authorities on Government policy on planning issues and as such is a material consideration in land-use decisions. This involves decisions on individual planning applications and appeals.

On the subject of recording buildings PPG15 makes it clear that the Royal Commission on the Historical Monuments of England must be notified of all proposals to demolish listed buildings, and be allowed access to them for the purposes of recording. It is within the powers of a planning authority to attach conditions that require applicants to arrange for suitable programmes of recording prior to any alterations or demolition work. In addition arrangements to record, and where appropriate retain, hidden features that only come to light during site works may also be the subject of a planning condition.

It is not within the power of planning authorities, however, to require applicants to finance such recording programmes in return for the granting of planning permission. Nor should applicants expect to be granted consent to alter or demolish listed buildings merely because they have arranged suitable recording programmes (PPG15, paragraph 3.23).

ASSESSING THE HERITAGE - HOW IMPORTANT IS IT?

There is considerable agreement between archaeologists and nature conservationists about how the value of heritage sites and areas should be assessed. For instance, the non-statutory criteria for scheduling monuments of national importance (DoE 1983) are closely related to those for assessing Sites of Special Scientific Interest. They also provide a useful starting point for the assessment of other heritage areas and sites. For scheduling monuments they are:

■ **Survival/condition.** The value of a monument is enhanced by good survival of archaeological potential.

■ **Period.** All types of monument that characterise a period should be considered for protection so that the surviving sample does not become biased.

■ **Rarity.** Selection must portray the commonplace and typical as well as the rare.

■ **Fragility/vulnerability.** Particularly fragile or vulnerable monuments should be given enhanced protection.

■ **Diversity.** Some monuments have a combination of high quality features; others have a single important attribute.

■ **Documentation.** Value is enhanced by the existence of records either contemporary with its use or of past investigations.

■ **Group value.** Value is enhanced by association with other monuments of the same or other periods.

■ **Potential.** The nature of the evidence cannot be precisely specified at present, but scheduling may be justified by its probable existence and importance.

It is worth noting that informational values dominate entirely - aesthetic, associative and symbolic values are not taken into account. However architectural conservation, as might be expected, places

English Heritage

Stockwell Bus Garage, London, an example of a post-war listed building designed by Adie, Button and Partners with Thomas Bilbow, was built by London Transport in 1950-54.

more emphasis on design aspects. This is illustrated by the criteria for listing buildings, where design takes a much more important role:

Period criteria

■ All buildings built before 1700 which survive in anything like their original condition.

■ Most buildings of 1700 to 1840, though selection is necessary.

■ Between 1840 and 1914 only buildings of 'definite quality and character'.

■ Between 1914 and 1939 selected buildings of high quality or historic interest.

■ A few outstanding buildings erected after 1939 (currently a very lively issue with the Department of National Heritage encouraging a debate on the listing of controversial buildings from the 1960s and 1970s).

Buildings are chosen for:

■ Special value within types, for architecture, planning or as illustrative of social or economic history.

■ Technological innovation or virtuosity.

■ Association with well-known characters or events.

■ Group value, especially as examples of town planning (eg squares, terraces, model villages). These lists, taken together, help to define the ways in which heritage conservers currently assess the value of these types of heritage.

Whatever the criteria, assessment inevitably involves making judgements. It is not an exact science and can never be wholly objective. For this reason, English Heritage has attempted as part of a major initiative known as the Monuments Protection Programme to devise ways of taking the approach further in dealing with the scheduling of monuments. A number of research projects have been set up, looking at known, recorded sites; sites recorded by aerial photography; industrial remains; urban areas; and landscapes in detail.

It is clear that there is a problem of definition: what is a 'site'? In deciding national importance, how can one judge together such disparate features as a single standing stone or barrow, a cropmark of buried ditches in a field of barley, or the whole of Fountains Abbey or the city of York? Equally, how can one balance the importance a site might have originally had to its makers against the importance it might now have because of its survival and modern condition? A further problem in assessing archaeological resources is that they are generally speaking buried, and therefore hidden from view. But assessing sites you cannot see and cannot fully understand without excavating (and therefore destroying) them is a difficult matter.

It should also be noted that the 1979 Ancient Monuments and Archaeological Areas Act refers to the scheduling of 'works' of man - could these include, for example, scatters of flints in a ploughed field, or coppiced ancient woodlands? At present the general view is that these are excluded.

All these criteria assume that the physical heritage can be defined on the ground. However this is not as easy as it might seem. Buildings have their 'curtilage'; and conservation areas as well as archaeological and nature conservation sites may not have clear, obvious boundaries to them. They probably only exist because of their wider landscape context. Once a line is drawn and areas have been designated, the very act of designation tends to devalue the surrounding land: by drawing a line, we have effectively said to the world that everything outside it is less important.

This problem has long been recognised in the field of landscape conservation, where there is the additional problem that landscapes are by their nature large areas, used and enjoyed by a great range of people in different ways and for different reasons. The Countryside Commission has therefore promoted a management planning approach, based on landscape assessment. This attempts to balance objective and subjective criteria and establish areas which can be shown to have a special character derived from their geology, vegetation, or traditional farming patterns. The aim is to draw attention to landscape qualities and provide a basis for policy making. A different way of dealing with the problem is represented by the Commission's Countryside Stewardship Scheme. This has attempted to target important types of landscape, such as heathland, riverside landscapes, coasts, upland moor, chalk and limestone grassland, or 'historic landscapes', without designating areas on the ground.

ENVIRONMENTAL ASSESSMENT

Despite the difficulties mentioned, some attempt has to be made to define those features that should be retained for future generations to enjoy, otherwise they will simply disappear. Environmental assessment is an important technique for ensuring that the likely effects of a new development are fully understood and taken into account before development is allowed to go ahead. This type of assessment is done reactively, precisely because a major new development is planned. Following the EU Directive of 27 June 1985 (85/337) which was implemented in England and Wales in 1988, specific types of major development project (known as Schedule A developments such as motorways, oil refineries and nuclear power stations) may not go ahead unless an

Environmental Assessment (EA) has been carried out first to determine the likely impact. EAs on Schedule A developments are mandatory and must be commissioned by the developer before any scheme proceeds. Furthermore there is an obligation to consult statutory consultees. For other types of development, known as Schedule B types, EAs are not mandatory but discretionary. In the UK, all Environmental Assessments must contain information on the likely significant effects of the project on 'human beings, flora, fauna, soil, water, air, climate, the landscape, the interaction of the foregoing, material assets, and the cultural heritage'. The EA is the process of information collection and evaluation. This leads to the production of an *Environmental Statement* (ES) which is the document that sets out the developer's own assessment of

Mike Corbishley

Harpley, Norfolk. This prehistoric burial mound is all that remains of a cemetery which has been ploughed away despite being protected as a scheduled ancient monument.

Mike Corbishley

St Osyth, Essex. A Roman farm is excavated ahead of gravel extraction by an archaeological team.

likely environmental effects. The ES should include a summary in non-technical language.

Environmental Assessment is a systematic procedure, first developed in the United States of America in the 1970s. It has benefits for the developer, because he/she can anticipate problems, improve the design, and avoid last-minute changes and delays, while for the planner there is the opportunity to influence design and make more informed decisions. On the negative side, few types of development are included in Schedule A, and the onus for commissioning and undertaking the assessment is left in the hands of the developer. There is also the need occasionally to carry out Strategic EAs that are concerned with policy or legislation rather than specific projects. While these can be of great value they are rarely undertaken.

SETTING PRIORITIES

Having identified and analysed the heritage features of a region or area, priorities must be set and appropriate arrangements made for management, bearing in mind not only the intrinsic importance of each feature or area, but also any external constraints. Priorities must acknowledge what is possible as well as what is desirable.

Without a strategic framework, pure opportunism will mean that the most important sites will never receive the attention they deserve. There is no limit to the resources which could be applied to heritage conservation if they were available, but in reality they are always limited. Setting priorities means that resources can be targeted and their use justified.

However, sometimes prioritisation can become an obstacle to effective conservation, if it results in missed opportunities. It is no use sacrificing the chance to benefit one area simply because there are other more important ones elsewhere if these cannot be assisted. A balance is therefore needed which allows for opportunism within a broad, flexible strategic framework.

CONSIDER ALTERNATIVES

PROJECT DESIGN

IS EA MANDATORY/DISCRETIONARY
(ie. Is this a Schedule A development?)

IF MANDATORY,
WHAT SHOULD IT COVER?

PREPARATION OF
ENVIRONMENTAL STATEMENT:
includes
Consultation
Description of project and the existing environment
Impact prediction
Impact significance
Proposals for mitigation
Participation

PROPOSALS

REVIEW PUBLISHED
ENVIRONMENTAL STATEMENT

MAKE DECISION

MONITOR PROJECT IMPACTS

Diagram showing the stages involved with Environmental Assessment

Richborough Roman site, Kent, the landing place for the Roman invasion by the Emperor Claudius in AD 43. In the background is a power station.

English Heritage

PROTECTING THE HERITAGE

There has been an increasing realisation in recent years that the principle of *sustainable development* applies to the whole heritage - not just the natural environment. Change must be accommodated, but managed in such a way as to ensure that we pass our heritage on in as good a condition as we can to future generations. This means identifying, recording, prioritising, and establishing a management regime. Usually, a policy of minimum maintenance is followed, to try to prevent attrition and retain the site or building in a stable state.

We have to recognise that future research interests as well as techniques for studying the heritage are likely to be very different to those which are current today. All we can do is attempt to conserve (as far as possible) a representative sample of what we have inherited, and document our decisions.

Because both cultures and environments are dynamic and subject to many conflicting pressures, the heritage values of a site or area must be weighed against other values which society in general, or particular interests, might wish to place on it. Conservation is a balancing act, a negotiated compromise which should seek to obtain the best management available in the circumstances of each case. This is not always easy. For instance in the case of the Somerset Levels, a wetland management scheme for one feature (Neolithic trackways) is disadvantageous for neighbouring and important wet meadows. Raised (high nutrient) water levels have contributed to an increase in *Juncus effusus* to the detriment of other desirable species. More fundamentally perhaps, should wetland sites such as this be preserved by introducing 'pumping regimes' which are clearly not sustainable?

Every site is therefore subject to constraints, which need early identification. It is also important, for the same reason, to establish clear objectives for conservation in each case, based on an earlier assessment of value previously made.

Margaret Cox

The Somerset Levels are peatlands of international importance because of their particular ecological composition. They illustrate some of the opportunities and problems of heritage conservation. Peat extraction has revealed Neolithic wooden trackways of enormous archaeological value preserved in the wet conditions; but peat extraction itself threatens the ecology of the area and is upsetting the habitat of migratory birds. Increasing co-operation is helping to ensure that management for archaeology and nature conservation is compatible. The traditional peat industry itself is also a valued heritage, both economically and socially. Recently the Royal Commission on the Historical Monuments of England has funded a survey of old peat cuttings on Shapwick Heath prior to their destruction.

LEGAL FRAMEWORKS AND DESIGNATION

Different aspects of the heritage have been legally designated in different ways:

Landscapes

Vernacular landscapes, which have changed and developed in response to peoples' needs over the centuries, may be *National Parks* (or equivalent designations like the Norfolk Broads), *Areas of Outstanding Natural Beauty* (AONBs), or *Heritage Coasts* - these come under the overall responsibility of the Countryside Commission. National Parks have their own management committees and staff who are expected to balance the needs of conservation with those of public access and enjoyment. They are (apart from the Norfolk Broads) upland areas considered to have an element of wildness and rugged charm to them.

AONBs are less formal in their structures and are for conservation only. These tend to be rolling chalk and limestone hills, and whereas the national parks are concentrated in the north and west of England, the AONBs are to be found more in the south and east.

In their own way and on a much smaller scale, Heritage Coasts try to achieve similar ends. They usually have a management committee made up of interested parties and a project officer to develop a work programme.

The Ministry of Agriculture Fisheries and Food and its Scottish and Welsh sister departments have designated *Environmentally Sensitive Areas*, as part of EU policy. These are areas of countryside where special grants are available to farmers and landowners to conserve the local environment and heritage, including archaeological sites and characteristic features such as field walls and hedges, by encouraging, through grant-aid, traditional farming practices. They are not the same as 'setaside' schemes where areas of arable land are left unfarmed, but are an incentive to promote less intensive farming methods in certain areas.

Habitats

Britain is now required to protect areas and species of European importance under the EU's Habitat and Species Directive. As of April 1995 Britain is the first EU member state to draw up a list of protected sites and species, lowland raised bogs, heathlands and Caledonian pine forests, which includes the otter and the greater horseshoe bat. In all nearly 300 sites have been proposed for the UK which are to be designated *Special Areas of Conservation*. Included in the proposed list of sites are Borrowdale Woods in Cumbria for its old oaks; Bredon Hill in Hereford and Worcester home of the violet click beetle; the Wash and north Norfolk coast for its salt meadows, mudflats and sand banks; Epping Forest in Essex for its beech trees and stag beetles; and Beinn Dearg in the Highlands for its Alpine heaths, grasslands and herbs.

Stricter legal controls will be enforced on these new reserves over projects such as road building, peat digging, fishing, and river barrages, and levels of pollution currently allowed in many rivers should be cut. Valued habitats are designated under the Wildlife and Countryside Act 1981 as *Sites of Special Scientific Interest* (SSSI) or National (or local) Nature Reserves. SSSIs are of national importance for either their wildlife or their geological interest. Ecological SSSIs are designated by English Nature, or its equivalent bodies in Scotland and Wales. Geological SSSIs are the responsibility of the UK-wide Joint Nature Conservancy Committee (JNCC).

Buildings and areas

Under the Town and Country Planning Acts, historic buildings are Listed by the Secretary of State and are graded I, II★ and II in England or Wales or A,B and C in Scotland and Northern Ireland. Their importance is assessed by English Heritage, Cadw, Historic Scotland, or the DoE (NI) respectively. Listing gives them legal protection through the planning system. Grade 1, Grade A listed buildings are of exceptional importance. *Conservation Areas* are established by local authorities in consultation with English Heritage or its equivalent bodies to protect groups of buildings, village or town centres.

Parks and gardens

Designed landscapes such as parks and gardens appear on non-statutory registers established by English Heritage, Historic Scotland or Cadw, and are also graded in the same way as listed buildings to draw attention to their importance.

Sites and monuments

Archaeological sites and monuments are covered by the Ancient Monuments and Archaeological Areas Act 1979. They are either *Scheduled* by the Secretary of State on the advice of English Heritage (or equivalent bodies in Scotland and Wales) as being of national importance; or they are deemed to be of local importance and left to local authorities to deal with through the planning system. Under the 1979 Act, either the Secretary of State or local authorities may negotiate arrangements for protective *Guardianship* of a site with its owners.

Shipwrecks

At sea, the remains of shipwrecks may be *Protected Wrecks*, granting legal protection to them, but at present very few are designated. *Marine Protected Areas* are another, separate designation.

World Heritage Sites

At the international level, the United Nations (UNESCO) designates *World Heritage Sites* for either their natural or cultural importance.

It is immediately obvious however that there is no overall, consistent approach in the UK to the legal protection of the heritage. Archaeological sites, historic buildings, nature conservation sites and landscapes are all covered by different legislation.

It could also be argued that to fence parts of the heritage off, (figuratively or literally) and hand them over to experts and bureaucrats is to divorce people's experience of the past from the present, to take it away and claim it exclusively for the specialist and the professional.

On the other hand, without a system of designation it would be difficult to make special provision for important and valued sites and areas. Designation provides at least official recognition of importance and an indication that policy will (or should) attempt to avoid destroying them.

BENEFICIAL MANAGEMENT

Where an area is owned or controlled by a sympathetic person or organisation, there may be opportunities for *beneficial management* aimed at achieving the objectives decided upon. The National Trust and the National Trust for Scotland, for example, have drawn up management plans for many of their estates. Often a policy of minimum intervention is proposed with the aim of preventing natural decay and retaining the site or area

Studley Royal, North Yorkshire. This eighteenth-century garden is now part of a World Heritage Site.

Mark Brisbane

as far as possible in the condition in which it was found.

If the objectives are primarily to conserve the information value of the site, and that information value is considered to lie in stratified deposits threatened by scrub or tree invasion (or the roots of planted trees) then clearance might be considered. However if the value of the site lies primarily in its vegetation - perhaps as part of a landscape design, or a habitat for wildlife - such an approach would obviously not be appropriate.

More difficult decisions may have to be made where the romantic effect of a ruin is enhanced by vegetation which is gradually destroying the stonework. Here the aesthetic considerations may have to give way to the need to stabilise the masonry, or the whole site (romantic effect included) could be jeopardised.

Sometimes a decision is made to restore a building, earthwork, garden or other feature to its appearance at a particular stage in its history. This can be of immense educational and research value as an experiment, but as it may remove the site's evidence for subsequent (and possibly its previous) history, cannot be undertaken lightly.

MANAGEMENT PLANNING

Increasingly, management plans are being prepared for sites, areas and landscapes of heritage value. These provide a framework for discussion, consultation and agreed action, and try to set out what the objectives and priorities are for conservation.

The first stage in management planning is to define, map and assess the area to be conserved, and to identify broad objectives. It is then essential to consider the constraints present to establish a framework of what is possible in practice. Current land-use and conflicts of interest for example may mean that compromises must be reached. Often there is a severe constraint of limited financial resources.

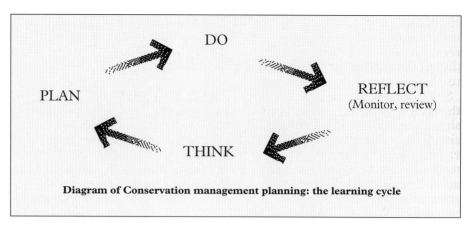

Diagram of Conservation management planning: the learning cycle

There may also be opportunities for obtaining benefits which might not otherwise have been considered, and identifying these can be a valuable part of the process. Then the various options open to the manager need to be set out and analysed. From these, proposals are drawn out for specific action, with a timetable of when works will be carried out. These proposals need to include arrangements for monitoring progress so that adjustments can be made to the programme if necessary; and for a regular, more thorough review of the plan itself and its implementation. Thus the process aims to provide for a learning cycle for those involved, so that conservation can be continually improved by experience.

As we have seen, conscious management decisions must be made - and justified. The demands of different conservation interests can complement or conflict with each other. Communication and understanding between conservationists themselves is therefore essential, leading to a need for facilitators as much as the traditional specialists.

At the same time, new techniques and possibilities for management action are constantly being developed. This is why effective and appropriate education is essential for those who wish to take a part in managing the heritage.

RESEARCH

Without research into the heritage, and also into improved methods for its care, new methods and approaches could not be developed. Conscious decisions may therefore be taken to exploit sites, buildings and areas for research or educational purposes. This must be done with extreme caution and to the highest possible standards, because the resource is finite and

At Kenwood House on London's Hampstead Heath, a sphagnum bog (classified as an SSSI) has been saved by the removal of birch and oak which grew after grazing and regular grass cutting were discontinued in the mid 1950s. The trees were providing too much shade for the sphagnum moss to survive.

subject to constant natural attrition, and because archaeological research - if done by excavation or dismantling of upstanding structures - is destructive.

Some people have argued that for these reasons no excavations should take place on archaeological sites which are otherwise unthreatened. However, modern excavation techniques allow increasing amounts of information to be recovered using minimal intervention. There is also a compelling counter-argument that research should be done in the most effective way to answer specific questions, and that sites for research should be selected for these reasons, not because they happen to be in danger. Further, if a site is not otherwise threatened, there remains an opportunity to check the results of an excavation in the future, by reopening the trenches (as has been done, for example, at Maiden Castle in Dorset and at Sutton Hoo, Suffolk). Unless the resource is used intelligently to improve our knowledge, its information values are lost.

EDUCATION

There has been a long tradition of using visits to museums and historic sites as part of teaching in schools. However, the introduction of the National Curriculum in English and Welsh schools has seen an increase in this use. The history curriculum requires that pupils are taught from a wide range of evidence, including artefacts, buildings and sites. The development of an evidence-based curriculum is discussed in detail in Corbishley and Stone, 1994.
Pupils in school are encouraged to look beyond the remains of ancient sites and to consider the management of sites open to the public as well as more general environmental concerns.
At more advanced levels, there is a wide range of courses for both full-time students and people attending continuing education classes. The General National Vocational Qualification has modules such as Travel and Tourism (*see Bibliography*) in which heritage sites should be studied. At both graduate and post-graduate levels there are a number of courses available which deal with cultural resource management.

ECONOMIC DEVELOPMENT

Where people value an object, building, or area for any reason, they are likely to want to see it, visit it, study it, even possess it. We have already seen how appealing the word 'heritage' is for advertisers, who use it to sell their products and services. It is for the consumer to decide whether these things are really of value to them or not.

More directly, heritage tourism and the international antiquities trade attempt to cater for some of the demands which arise from the other heritage values. The heritage therefore enters the marketplace. As in any market, thefts sometimes take place, false claims are sometimes made and genuine values are sometimes debased by fake ones.

However it would be completely wrong to dismiss every serious attempt to interpret, enjoy, or understand the heritage merely because of the tawdry and the frivolous - just as it would be to dispose of a whole library of valuable books because the library happened also to contain some worthless material.

Furthermore, there has been an undeniable benefit to the heritage from the tourist industry which has acted as a catalyst, and sometimes a direct stimulus, for the restora-

RIGHT: Maiden Castle, Dorset. Excavations conducted by an English Heritage team.

BELOW: Wroxeter Roman City. Studying materials and their properties is part of National Curriculum science work for primary school pupils.

tion of historic buildings and the preservation of sites and monuments. Tourism is frequently cited as the reason for local authority support for historic towns, monuments and the countryside, and places that have no 'unique selling point' are busy trying to manufacture one from less promising material. Then there is the income from the tourists themselves, income which is vitally important to organisations like the National Trust and the members of the Historic Houses Association, as well as to the infrastructure of hotels, restaurants, and so on.

On the other hand, commercialisation of the heritage can produce very real conflicts between the economic and the other values a site, area, or artefact may have. The

English Heritage

Roger White

evidence, aesthetic, or wildlife value of a place may be damaged just as much by inaccurate or uncritical presentation as by the trampling and damage caused by visitors.

Facilities for tourism - hotels, restaurants, shops, transport infrastructure - with their associated requirements for power, water supplies and waste disposal - can destroy the atmosphere and ambience, as well as the historic context of a place. Indeed visitors themselves may cause destructive processes just by being there. At Lascaux in France, visitors may now only visit a replica of the original caves with their wonderful collection of Palaeolithic art. The original had to be protected from their breath which changed the balance of oxygen, carbon dioxide and water vapour in the air, causing the deterioration of the paintings.

Equally, visitors' feet have eroded the floors of English and French cathedrals like York, Canterbury, Chartres and Notre Dame and major churches like Westminster Abbey. The number of visitors to these sites is enormous and shows no sign of declining significantly. For instance, it has been estimated that Notre Dame cathedral received a staggering 10.5 million visits in 1989, more than any tourist destination in Paris, and this number is expected to grow to 13 million in the near future.

One of the most dangerous aspects of commercialisation in heritage tourism is its frequent lack of concern for accuracy and criticism. In the late 1980s so-called heritage centres sprang up, purporting to entertain (and sometimes to educate) the visitor. Although some were excellent, others were purely commercial ventures, which exhibited a taste for uncritical nostalgia. Where little attention is paid to involving people actively in exploring and understanding their heritage, such attractions can sometimes present an unbalanced view which leaves visitors with the impression that their past has been taken from them, packaged, commercialised, and removed of all meaning.

Visitors continue to frequent the London Dungeon much as people continue to go to horror films - with no very serious expectation that life was really like this. Theme parks are seen to have more in common with the funfair than the museum. As with films, publishing, or other media, we must now expect a range of products - as newspapers range from the Sunday Times to the Sunday Sport.

The antiquities trade is another field which has brought criticism of the heritage. Lack of international regulation has led to fraud, deception and theft. Sites are looted, works of art stolen, and much of the value of the artefacts is lost as they are taken out of context. Unfortunately London seems to be one of the centres for this worldwide activity (Greenfield, 1990).

ABOVE: The Wrekin, Shropshire. People with metal detectors frequently pillage this pre-Roman Celtic settlement despite it being a scheduled ancient monument.

BELOW: The Canterbury Tales, in Canterbury. Visitors can experience parts of Chaucer's stories in a recreation of medieval settings which have been carefully researched from archaeological and documentary evidence.

Canterbury	2,250,000
York	2,250,000
St Paul's	1,400,000
Salisbury	550,000
Winchester	500,000
St Albans	400,000
Wells	391,000
Lincoln	375,000
Durham	365,000
Ely	200,000

Visitor figures for some of England's most popular cathedrals in 1992.

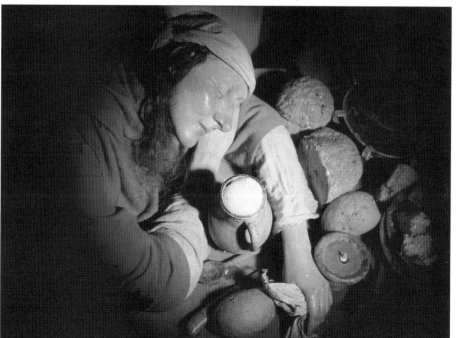

INTERPRETING THE HERITAGE

Heritage not only requires preservation and protection, but also interpretation. If a building, artefact, or archaeological site warrants preserving, it also needs interpreting so that its meaning can be more widely understood and appreciated. Explaining its value and significance to a wide and differing audience which may include schoolchildren, foreign visitors, casual day-trippers, or academic specialists is as fundamentally important as preserving and protecting it. Like preservation and protection, a framework is needed in which to undertake such an important task. This section will examine that framework together with some of the aims and general approaches to interpretation.

DEFINING INTERPRETATION

First, what is meant by interpretation? Put simplistically, it is primarily about explaining the meaning of something. But of course the same thing may mean different things to different people and as we have already seen because the heritage is a part of people's past it is a very complex, sometimes subjective and often personalised subject. The vantage point of the viewer and that of the interpreter are all-important.

The same human skeleton stored in a museum collection may be interpreted one way by a human bone specialist ('during life this person suffered from arthritis'), one way by an archaeologist ('this skeleton comes from a sixteenth century grave mound') and yet another way by a Native American ('this is an ancestor of my people and should be returned to the homeland and re-buried'). All three views may be equally valid but represent very different approaches to the same entity and would lead to very different interpretations.

Right at the outset it is important to recognise that different views do exist and will inevitably affect the way a part of the heritage is inter-

preted. These differences may be due to the type and level of expertise of the interpreter or to his/her preconceived ideas or prejudices about the subject matter being interpreted, its historical context or its intended audience. Any of these differences may well lead the eventual interpretation to be biased in some way. Alternatively, Peter Rumble makes the point that although interpretation is almost always selective and incomplete, 'the accurate presentation from a single point of view can be justified provided it leads on to a consideration of the totality' (Rumble, 1989, 30).

Of course it may be possible to remove some bias by attempting to ensure that the interpreter has no particular axe to grind and is emotionally uninvolved with the subject matter. Unfortunately, such independence may produce bland interpretation by removing some of the vitality and enthusiasm of the expert or the emotionally charged vision of the active participant. Furthermore, the arbiter's so-called 'independent' act of deciding to leave out information is in itself a form of bias. Like journalism, interpretation requires editing. It is not usually possible to cover every single aspect and detail, nor would one wish to, hence the introduction of selectivity. And herein lies one of

the biggest problems facing anyone involved with interpreting: what to include and what to exclude.

Another problem concerns understanding: what is an appropriate style and complexity of language to use for an audience? The key point here is being able to define the audience so that interpretation is matched, as far as possible, to their needs and their level of knowledge. Often heritage is interpreted without acknowledging who the interpretation is for, what it is trying to do, or how the interpreter has gone about doing it. An ill thought out approach will produce problems both for the interpreter and the audience. For instance when an archaeologist talks in a technical, jargon-laden way about an excavation of a Neolithic henge monument, the general public will almost certainly be confused about both the meaning and the significance of the site.

To avoid this confusion, interpretation needs careful planning and execution if it is to be successful. It must have clear aims and objectives, which first of all must be agreed with the entire team involved in the project and should then be made explicit to the audience so that they can share in the interpreters' reasons for including or excluding certain facts or suppositions about the subject matter.

Visitors and interpretation panels at Maiden Castle, Dorset, an English Heritage site. Displays of the material found during excavations at the hillfort are located nearby in Dorchester at Dorset County Museum.

STAGES IN INTERPRETATION

The following are the main stages in the interpretation process:

■ Pre-planning / front-end research:

Visitor potential
Visitor profile
Visitor expectations
Visit pre-knowledge
Carrying capacity of the site

■ Planning:

Assembling the team
Setting the aims
Defining the audience
Defining the site
Determining the message
Identifying resources
Defining linkages to a marketing strategy
Formulating a timetable using appropriate techniques, such as critical path analysis
Writing a brief

■ Choosing the type of interpretation:

Identifying the target audience
Setting objectives
Deciding on appropriate level of interpretation, such as reading age
Deciding on presentational techniques

■ Undertaking the interpretation itself:

Sticking to the brief: were changes in keeping with the original aims?
Achieving completion on time and on budget

■ Marketing the site and storyline:

Reaching the target audience
Use of appropriate marketing techniques

■ Evaluating:

Has it attracted an audience?
Were they the target audience?
Does it fulfil audience expectations?
What was the visitor reaction?
Did it get the message across?

■ Feedback:

Based on the evaluation, what improvements does the interpretation require?
What lessons have been learnt for the next time?

Another fundamental factor that influences how heritage is interpreted is the management philosophy that lies behind the organisation that is preserving and presenting that heritage. As we have seen in previous chapters, heritage may be preserved for a variety of reasons by people motivated in different ways. If economic success as measured by visitor numbers and income is the primary aim of the organisation, then it is likely that site interpretation is market driven to attract maximum visitors. This can easily lead to the site being exploited via sensationalism as a matter of expediency. If, on the other hand, motivation derives from an appreciation of the integrity and value of the site or artefact collection itself, and a desire to present aspects of it to a wider audience while preserving it for posterity then a rather different interpretational model may be developed.

In practice interpretation, through the selection of appropriate messages and media, seeks a balance that suits both site constraints and management objectives.

One of the first and most respected of early interpreters was Freeman Tilden, who wrote the now classic textbook on interpretation entitled *Interpreting Our Heritage* in 1957. In it he set out six principles which can be summarised as follows:

■ Information on its own is not interpretation

■ Any interpretation that does not somehow relate what is being displayed or described to something within the personality or experience of the visitor will be sterile

■ Interpretation is an art, whether the materials being presented are scientific, historical, architectural, or environmental

■ The chief aim of interpretation is not instruction, but provocation

■ Interpretation should aim to present a whole rather than a part

Visitors to the doll collection at the Museum of Lakeland Life & Industry, Kendal.

English Heritage

28

■ Interpretation for children should not be a dilution of the presentation to adults, but should develop its own approach.

Tilden developed these ideas after years of practical experience working with the US National Park Service, interpreting the natural world for thousands of visitors. He believed that interpretation was fundamentally an educational activity which aimed to reveal meanings and relationships through the use of original objects, illustrative media and firsthand experience. It was, for him, much more than communicating factual information.

WHY INTERPRET?

The Society for the Interpretation of Britain's Heritage (SIBH), known as Interpret Britain, have described interpretation as:

"the process of explaining to people the significance of the place or object they have come to see, so that they enjoy their visit more, understand their heritage and environment better, and develop a more caring attitude to conservation."

This is a very specific set of aims for interpreting heritage, which has the added advantage of being measurable in terms of success. That is, has the interpretation enhanced the visitors' experience, helped their understanding, and created a better awareness about the conservation issues associated with certain relevant aspects of the heritage?

Visitor enjoyment and understanding lie at the heart of interpretation, although this can be implemented rather differently from place to place. For instance, minimal interpretation may be used in order to allow the visitor to relate directly with a place, a landscape or a work of art. Enjoyment comes from the personal experience of feeling an emotional response and the understanding may be as much about self-understanding as about the place or object being experienced.

Alternatively, substantial amounts of information may be presented in any number of different ways combining leaflets, booklets, display panels, video presentations, or audio cassettes for personal stereos: all of which depend on visitors self-

English Heritage

guiding themselves through a place. Enjoyment comes partly through discovery and finding out more about a place, an object, or the past generally.

Other approaches may rely on guided tours, some by interpreters in appropriate historical costume. These may be developed still further by the use of so-called 'living history' where the objective is to re-create past ways of life as realistically as possible. Living history events can be lively and exciting if done well, offering the visitor an experience of the past through drama, re-enactments or demonstrations. Some interpreters will even 'stay in period' refusing to acknowledge late twentieth century technology nor language. These are not easy interpretations to undertake as authenticity can so easily be compromised. There are a number of groups who specialise in re-enactments including the Ermine Street Guard, the English Civil War Society and specialist companies such as Past Pleasures who undertake living history events from a number of periods.

These various approaches to interpretation are attempting to enhance the experience of the visitor by aiding understanding, heightening awareness of surroundings or increasing the visitor's personal involvement with some aspect of the heritage. There is however an active philosophical debate about how valid certain forms of interpretation actually are. Can living history, for instance, ever represent the past and will it really help people to understand it? There is often a fine line between

Bolsover Castle, Derbyshire. Music in keeping with the monument from the group called Hautbois.

explanation and over-elaboration or exploitation. Some heritage venues have been accused of making it more 'real' than it really was. In other words, creating a simulacrum, a deceptive image of the past, a sham.

This has been described as attempting to create an exact imitation of something that never existed. At Colonial Williamsburg, Virginia, the difference between restoration and re-creation is deliberately confused: the visitor unable to determine easily what is genuinely old and what only appears to be old.

Some of these general comments on interpreting sites apply equally to interpreting objects and collections, usually in a museum context. What is the primary motivating force behind the display of objects? The museological motivation for exhibiting is to present to the visitor objects from the museum's collection together with the necessary information so that learning can occur. David Dean (1994, 2) has discussed secondary goals for museum exhibitions. These are:

■ Promoting community interest in the museum by offering alternative leisure activities where individuals or groups may find worthwhile experiences.

■ Supporting the institution financially: exhibitions help the museum as a whole justify its existence and its expectation of continued support.

■ Providing proof of responsible handling of collections if a donor wishes to give objects. Properly presented exhibitions confirm public trust in the museum as a place for conservation and careful preservation.

Exhibitions may enhance the credibility of a museum amongst its local supporters and a wider audience which includes non-local visitors and members of the museum community.

Different organisations will therefore have different reasons for presenting objects and information to the public. Nevertheless, at the heart of interpretation should lie a fundamental desire to explain and enthuse so that members of the public might be moved, excited or provoked about some aspect of the heritage.

DETERMINING THE AUDIENCE

Who is it for?

Who goes to see the heritage and what motivates visitors to go in the first place?

A simple listing of the visitor figures gives some idea of the popularity of visiting the past as a leisure pursuit.

■ In 1987 in the UK there were 145 million visits to 2,666 heritage attractions, as defined and compiled by the British Tourist

Authority. This figure includes some 57 million visits to museums and galleries.

■ In 1989, there were over 70 million visits to art galleries and museums and the museum business was running at such a pace that it was said at the time that a new museum opened in Britain once a fortnight.

■ By 1992, the British Tourist Authority's figures suggested that nearly 80 million visits to 1,759 museums and galleries took place, although a separate, much more detailed survey conducted by the Museums and Galleries

Commission indicated that a more accurate figure was probably around 110 million visits (Davies, 1994, 36).

It is sometimes easy to forget that historic sites and museums were not always there to be visited and even when they were people were not always encouraged to come. Although many owners of great houses allowed small numbers of visitors to tour their homes (Horace Walpole had strict limits

BELOW: Framlingham Castle, Suffolk. Events arranged by English Heritage can increase the number of visitors to rural sites.

English Heritage

Tourist Attractions			Visits	(in millions)		
	1988	1989	1990	1991	1992	% Change (1988-92)
Museums/galleries	70.4	71.1	75.3	76.1	79.2	12.5
Historic buildings	64.3	66.9	68.3	65.7	65.7	2.2
Country parks	41.3	45.4	47.7	49.2	48.2	16.7
Theme/leisure parks	34.4	36.8	37.6	36.9	36.5	6.1
Wildlife attractions	23.3	24.4	25.2	24.2	21.6	-7.3
Gardens	12.6	14.2	14.5	15.2	15.2	20.6
Workplaces	9.7	10.1	10.3	10.1	10.2	5.2
Steam railways	4.8	5.1	5.1	5.0	4.8	0.0
Other	55.0	57.6	60.9	59.0	63.5	15.5
All attractions	315.8	331.6	344.9	341.4	344.9	9.2
% change year on year	-	5.0	4.0	-1.0	1.0	

Tourist attractions by visits (after Davies, 1994, 29).

The British Museum, London, which has seen a steady growth in its visitor numbers from 2.9 million in 1982 to 6.7 million in 1992.

of only four persons a day, if booked in advance, and no children) this would effectively be limited to 'people of means'. Visitors were taken on tour of the house by the housekeeper and the grounds by the gardener. This was often a lucrative sideline, especially for the housekeeper who might make between one shilling and half-a-crown a time. Writing of his housekeeper at Strawberry Hill in 1783, Horace Walpole declared that she had made such sums of money 'that I have a mind to marry her, and so repay myself that way for what I have flung away to make my house quite uncomfortable to me' (cited in Tinniswood, 1989, 97).

A literary example which shows

something of the manner and decorum of country house visiting in the early ninteenth century occurs in *Pride and Prejudice*, where Jane Austen describes the visit to Pemberley, the fine country house of Mr Darcy, by Elizabeth Bennet and her family. They are conducted through the rooms by the housekeeper and met by the gardener at the hall door for a tour of the grounds.

Occasionally, it was the intention from the outset to allow visitors to view a house and its grounds. This was the case at Castle Howard in Yorkshire, where the Earl of Carlisle realised that he had created not only a great house but also a landscaped setting for a grand

monument, part private and part public. Kedleston Hall near Derby is another example where Nathaniel Curzon, 1st Baron Scarsdale, employed Robert Adam to create a Palladian mansion set in a classical park landscape.

The early history of museums in this country shows them also to be elitist in their views of the general public and their role in instructing and educating. The British Museum which opened in 1759 did not at first encourage visitors, requiring pre-booked appointments: admission was by ticket only and these took several weeks and at least two trips to the Museum to obtain. Children were not allowed and proper attire was required (Alexander, 1979).

During the latter half of the nineteenth century the number of museums grew, encouraged by local authorities and philanthropists who saw a connection between museum collections, education and civic pride. Curiously, the educational role of museums in this country languished for a time during the earlier part of this century and it was not until the 1970s that museums, largely through local authority assistance, began to appoint Education Officers within museums with the specific remit to make the collections more accessible to schoolchildren and adult learners alike; the latter no doubt in part due to the growth of adult education generally through the work of the WEA, university extra-mural departments and the Open University.

The emphasis within today's National Curriculum on primary evidence has on the whole broadened the appeal of museums and heritage sites for use by teachers and schoolchildren, particularly at primary school level.

However, a duality in the purpose of museums still exists today. On the one hand the collection is paramount and its preservation in perpetuity must be maintained by setting and achieving high standards of collection care. On the other hand, curators know that the collection is there to be used and appreciated, studied and enjoyed, using up-to-date methods and techniques of interpretation, provided that no harm is done to the objects in the museum's care.

More than any other type of institution concerned with preservation,

Tourist Attractions	Visits (in millions)	
	1993	1994
Museums/galleries	66	67
Historic properties	58	58
Gardens	13	12.8
Zoo/safari parks	19	18.8
Other attractions (eg Country parks etc)	136	150.3

Source: English Heritage Monitor (published by the English Tourist Board)

museums have had a long time to consider the question of who their visitors are and what their needs might be. In the early twentieth century a small number of learned committees conducted periodic reviews of the role of museums. One of these was the British Association for the Advancement of Science who, in 1920, examined the link between museums and education and stated that the general public represented 'the vast majority of visitors to the public museums; we may safely regard them as having little or no special knowledge, and a very large proportion of them enter the museum without any specific purpose. They are just 'looking round''.

The introduction of a more statistically based approach to determining who visits museums was introduced in the United States and Canada in the 1950s and early 1960s. One of the pioneers was the Milwaukee Public Museum which collected information on their visitors and discovered how much their composition changed throughout the year (half their visitors in the summer were tourists, while in the winter less than a quarter were; in the summer ten to nineteen year olds made up one-third of their visitors, but over half in the winter; over 40% in the winter were college educated, but only around 20% in the summer). Figures of this kind can be used in a very specific way for a museum to orientate its subject matter, displays and type of interpretation to meet its changing visitor profile.

In the UK the Ulster Museum was one of the first to undertake regular surveys to ascertain who went to the Museum and this was followed by many other museums in the 1970s such as Leicester, Norwich, and Manchester. However there exists a fine balance between knowing or categorising your audience and stereotyping or labelling people with personal prejudice, letting unhelpful bias get in the way. Nevertheless, it is certainly true that the audience for heritage related sites and venues needs to be analysed to ensure that the most receptive audiences are targeted and to maximise the use of resources.

Castle Acre Castle, Norfolk. A school visit to the castle organised as part of National Curriculum history work.

The concept of *market segmentation* is developed from product marketing, but is equally important to marketing heritage attractions because most organisations need to focus resources and activity on the one or more market segments which are most appropriate to meeting their aims and objectives. While there are differences between the commercial sector and the heritage sector, it is still possible and desirable to breakdown visitors into categories based on demographics (usually by age, gender, class, and educational background), lifestyle, geography (usually by local residents, day trippers, and tourists), schools and special interest. For an example of a survey conducted along these lines for the museum sector, see Davies, 1994, especially pp. 50-61.

Why do people visit?

There is less information on those who do not visit heritage attractions. Knowing who does not come is crucially important for any organisation economically tied to visitor numbers. Whether for purely marketing reasons or due to an altruistic desire to reach a part of the local community who currently sees no reason for a visit, identifying the non-visitor and the reasons for not visiting will be particularly important in order to extend or change the visitor profile.

Marilyn Hood's study of why people choose not to visit museums determined that there were six criteria that influenced how people select leisure-time activities (Hood, 1983).

These are:

■ being with other people

■ doing something worthwhile

■ feeling comfortable and at ease

■ challenging new experiences

■ having the opportunity to learn

■ participating actively.

A recent survey by McManus who examined why people went to the Science Museum in London showed that approximately 20% came because they wanted an enjoyable day out with the family and another 20% gave recreation as their main reason for being there. Such feelings affect the manner in which visitors are open to any communication presented to them. About half of the sample she studied held expectations related to the educational mission of the museum. In all about 65% stated that the main hopes that they had for their visit required a satisfactory communication from and with the displays (another 22% said they came to have fun!). Upon arrival, visitors were therefore highly motivated, but this was not necessarily focussed in a studious and academic manner (McManus, 1991).

To conclude, museums have been interested for some time in determining who uses them and why. Even so it is difficult to deduce general principles about visitor motivation especially if the context

English Heritage

is broadened to include the range of heritage sites from archaeological excavations to country houses and national parks. While individual organisations, such as English Heritage and the National Trust, have data about their current membership and visitors, many sites and museums have information in a very general form and it is probably not precise enough for determining the future requirements of individual sites.

Distribution of UK adult population and museum and art gallery visitors, by class groups, in 1991

Class	% UK adult population	% Museum and art gallery visitors
A/B	19	28
C1	23	27
C2	28	24
D	17	13
E	13	8
Total	100	100

(after Davies, 1994, 56).

Visitors queuing outside the British Museum, London.

Dover Castle, Kent. English Heritage encourages adult education groups to visit their sites as part of study programmes.

Reasons for not visiting in three Isle of Wight museums

	Cowes Maritime Museum %	Newport Roman Villa %	Sandown Geology Museum %
Never heard of it	38	17	31
No time	26	35	31
Not interested	16	24	28
Other	20	24	10
Base (actual figures)	458	315	245

(after Davies, 1994, 67: Source: Isle of Wight Cultural Services, visitor survey, 1992).

DESIGNING INTERPRETATION

Once it is established by survey or other means who goes to a particular heritage site, or in the case of a new venture who is likely to go to that type of site, then interpretation can be developed for that target audience. In the case of a museum this may manifest itself in an exhibition policy and it is certainly the case that these days more and more museums and some heritage sites have a written policy covering interpretation and user services as part of their general management plans. These policies are influenced by a number of factors and include the following:

■ the collection/site itself: what does it have to offer?

■ the building or site: its location and its limitations in terms of space

■ the visitors themselves: their profile and behaviour

■ the views of the organisation's funding body

■ the availability of finance, staff time and expertise

■ specialist input from curators, interpreters, conservators, designers, and educationalists.

Underpinning these factors should be an understanding of community needs and expectations. A common mistake in interpretation is to make decisions on what and how to interpret based upon assumptions about community needs rather than on real information gathered from the community itself. For certain types of heritage-related venues, these community needs will be absolutely essential for survival, let alone success.

Having decided to undertake the task of interpreting, how does one create an effective exhibition? Certain basic prerequisites will need to be determined. These include:

■ Is the interpretation driven by the physical remains or by the ideas and concepts that are to be explained?

■ What are the explicit objectives of the interpretation and what effects should these have on the visitors? For instance is the intention to impart information, provoke an emotional response, obtain public sympathy, fund raise for a cause, encourage people to reminisce or a combination of these responses.

■ What is the storyline and how should it be phrased? In what order should information be given to visitors and at what level of detail? This will depend largely on the reading level of the intended visitors, but also on their ability to comprehend and remember what may be quite difficult for the non-specialist. Details on visitor composition will help here. It may be that if family groups include older members who can assist with interpretation for younger members this may be used as a resource when explaining events or objects from the recent past. Furthermore, it has been shown that family groups learn well.

■ Does the interpretation make the visitor work unnecessarily hard? Understanding new and sometimes complicated information is not easy at the best of times and the visitor is not in the comfort of their own home reading a book, but standing (almost certainly) surrounded by a variety of images all competing for his or her attention. Too much information, especially in the form of text, may be very off-putting for many people.

■ Does the visitor know where to go next? A basic point, but very important nonetheless. Visitors should not feel lost and should therefore be given guidance to assist them to get the most from the site. Visitor orientation is a key factor affecting their enjoyment and satisfaction and is best provided through a combination of good signposting, maps, plans and helpful staff.

■ Does the interpretation encourage any response or feedback from the visitor? Involving the visitor in this way may lead to greater satisfaction as well as better understanding.

In addition to these points, there are aspects of the way in which people normally behave when faced with displays and exhibitions in museums, art galleries, historic houses, and heritage centres that will affect the degree of success for the interpretation. This behaviour will need to be taken into account when assessing effective interpretation. We have already mentioned one or two of these behavioural patterns such as that family groups tend to learn well. Another aspect of group behaviour is that couples are more likely to proceed around an exhibition separately, and to discuss what they have seen afterwards. Visitors who come on their own are 50% more likely to read labels and panels thoroughly than those who come with others. Small groups of adults tend to have one member who leads, reads panels and labels, and interprets for the

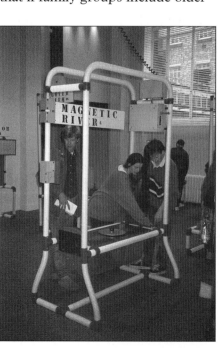

ABOVE: Colchester's Castle Museum. New displays combine the 'traditional' glass cases with recreations of structures from the past based on archaeological evidence.

RIGHT: Launch Pad, a hands-on interactive gallery at the Science Museum, London.

others, emphasising that social interaction within the group is the main focus of activity, not individual learning. Children, obviously, are more likely to try out the interactive parts of the display, and have less inhibitions about using computers and new technology. But in a survey at the Science Museum in London, it was also shown that females were more likely to play with interactive displays than males (McManus, 1991).

Another aspect of visitor behaviour is the impact that the exit has on the duration of a visit. Visitors give most attention to displays they encounter first and progressively less attention as they approach the exit. This was first realised as long ago as 1935 when Melton, writing about museums and art galleries, went so far as to say that 'the amount of attention received by an object is a function of its distance from the exits' (Melton, 1935, 93).

TYPES OF PRESENTATION

Presentations, predominately displays and exhibitions, may take a number of forms depending on the way in which they wish to present material and the theme they wish to pursue.

Didactic

A didactic display is one that is intended and designed to instruct. Its primary aim is the imparting of information. Part of the motivation behind a didactic display is the belief that knowledge is morally good, and that it helps to create well-informed people and responsible citizens. Its origins lie in the Protestant work ethic and the Victorian belief in self betterment that lay behind the creation of many public art galleries and museums in the nineteenth century.

Evolutionary

This puts objects, buildings or ideas into a chronological sequence, and may well emphasise the changes that occur through time. A consequence of this, whether intentional or unintentional, may be to imply that change equates with progress and that things improve as time goes by. May also be termed linear in approach.

On-site panels at this English Heritage site, Acton Burnell Castle in Shropshire, include text and illustrations.

Functional

A functional display puts the emphasis on how things work; what they do or did. Particularly dominate in technological and scientific displays, as well as in the general interpretation of industrial archaeology. May also stress the functional way in which humans deal with problems. Unlike an evolutionary approach, it stresses how people adapt to changing situations and environments: change is not simply a matter of progress through time.

Aesthetic

The intention of an aesthetic display is to emphasise the beauty of an object, a landscape or a building. This may explicitly or implicitly play upon the emotions of the visitor, taking advantage of the fascination with the ancient, the exotic and the beautiful.

Historical

Concentrates on what happened in the past, focussing on people and events: the role of individuals in making things happen.

Art historical

Concentrates on explaining the significance of aspects of the heritage in terms of style and fashion.

Economic

Concentrates on production and distribution: the relationship between people and objects through manufacture, trade and exchange.

Social

Explains the past through the links between people, places and objects. It is the relationship of these to the structure of society that gives meaning.

No matter which of the above (or more realistically which combination of the above) is used, the presentation will still not be fully objective, but at least its approach may be made explicit. Like an opera or a film, its success will depend partly on its content, but equally on the extent to which its perceptions and expressions are convincing for the audience.

APPROACHES TO INTERPRETATION

The approach to heritage interpretation will be largely dependent on some of the factors discussed in the preceding sections, but it is worth remembering that part of the definition of interpretation is concerned with explaining the significance of a site. This significance may well be dependent on the site's location as much as on its intrinsic value. For instance a small heathland on the edge of a large city may have a greater interpretive potential than an extensive moorland far removed from a centre of population. The value of a site such as this in educational and recreational terms is obviously enhanced by its accessibility and may well have the active support of the community who are willing to participate in its interpretation and conservation.

But how far should interpretation go? At what point does conservation end and restoration begin? These are more than academic questions because they go straight to the heart of one of the main debates in worldwide conservation today. The British view on conservation, and one largely followed in western Europe, is that limited intervention by specialist conservators is usually best, the so-called 'restore as found' philosophy. This limited intervention does not imply that specialists do little to ensure the survival of a site, monument or object, but that maintaining its integrity and its setting is paramount.

For instance, how much restoration work is appropriate at a ruined castle site? If it will aid the understanding of the site, should parts of fallen walls be put back? What materials are appropriate to use in this restoration work? And if we are uncertain about any part of the original design is it ever justifiable to recreate what we think it might have looked like?

These are issues which regularly confront professionals working in the various areas of conservation,

John Wood

Eilean Donan castle, Highland region, Scotland. The castle was largely rebuilt between 1912 and 1932 in a Victorian Romantic style, obliterating much of the original.

be they artefact conservators, archaeologists, conservation officers in local government, historic building architects, country house managers, interpreters or designers. They concern the ethics that lie behind the day to day practical solutions to problems that need to be confronted. To assist them in their work, many can turn to professional Codes of Ethics or Codes of Practice which will offer general principles based upon current best practice and the collective knowledge of each profession.

And what about the landscape? What maintenance regimes and interpretation models should be used knowing that different solutions will lead to certain plants and species being either encouraged or discouraged or that other conflicts may arise between the needs of the visitor and the needs of the habitat. Indeed there may often be occasions when the needs of the flora and fauna are directly in conflict with the needs of the built environment or cultural remains (tree root damage to archaeological sites is a common example of this).

When it comes to presenting and resolving these matters, there are two important historical strands to acknowledge because it is from

them that part of this century's countryside interpretation has developed. The first of these was the development in the United States of the concept of the National Park, the first one to be created being Yellowstone in 1872, and the subsequent establishment of the US National Park Service in 1916, which became the leading innovator of landscape and wilderness interpretation.

The other strand is very much a European one, and largely Scandinavian, having its origins in the Folk Museum (the first opened in Oslo in 1881) and the Swedish development of the open-air country life museum. The first of these was Skansen Open Air Museum in Stockholm conceived by Artur Hazelius in 1878 and opened in

1891. Interestingly, it was the development of these museums with their reconstructions of past or passing lifestyles which greatly influenced John D Rockefeller Jnr who went back to the USA and set up Colonial Williamsburg in Virginia. This concept of reconstruction was then developed at many other historic sites in the United States where the past was recreated at colonial settlement sites such as Dearborn and Old Sturbridge Village.

What are some of the options available to conservators and interpreters?

Restore in situ
The usual practice undertaken by major heritage organisations such as English Heritage, Cadw and Historic Scotland. This will use original materials wherever possible and use modern methods of consolidation and repair, but will not recreate (see below). The specialisms of archaeology (on both below and above ground remains), documentary research, and historic building conservation are essential. In the case of historic gardens and landscapes, archaeological research can be as important as documentary research.

Remove and re-erect
Sometimes it is not possible to maintain or save something in its original position and its removal is the only alternative to destruction. This can apply to wildlife and

English Heritage

Old Sarum, near Salisbury, Wiltshire. A traditional (minimalist) approach to the conservation and interpretation of ruins.

A building after re-erection at the Weald and Downland Open Air Museum, Singleton, West Sussex

Part of the Lunt Roman fort, near Coventry, has been re-created after excavation.

plants as well as buildings, monuments, or even historic street furniture (for example, a nineteenth century water pump and horse trough re-sited due to an urban road widening scheme). However, perhaps the most common type of feature that this applies to is buildings re-located to an Open Air Museum such as the Weald and Downland Open Air Museum in Singleton, West Sussex or the Avoncroft Museum of Buildings in Bromsgrove, Hereford and Worcester. Both of these museums were established in the 1960s as a response to the intense threat to historic vernacular buildings caused by widespread and often unchecked development, where removal to the safety of the museum was the only viable alternative. The motivation behind these two museums was preservation together with an intense academic interest in the buildings themselves, their history and development.

Relocation of buildings onto one site offers enormous scope for interpretation, allowing close examination of building styles and materials together with related craft activities. Today, however, the re-use of such buildings is more likely than their removal, the advantage here being that even though the original use may be lost, the setting and context of the building will remain.

There are other well known examples that go further than the two mentioned above and which blur the distinction between a straightforward re-erection of something from the past and its use

in a wider reconstruction of that past. An example of this is the North of England Open Air Museum at Beamish, County Durham, founded in 1970. Here on a 200 acre site of mainly farmland and woods have been erected a variety of buildings from miners' cottages to a railway station, an urban street scene, a colliery, and a number of shops, all linked together by a tramline. Although actors are not usually used to enliven the displays further, attendants are dressed in period costume.

Beamish has been criticised, perhaps somewhat unfairly, for portraying a past that never existed and, worse still, portraying this through real objects and buildings, thus making it seem more real than it ever was, and infinitely more cosy than today's hectic and quickly changing pattern of life

(Hewison, 1987). It is a prime example of what has been termed the nostalgic view of the past: one that only exists in period dramas made for television. It is perhaps no coincidence that sites like Beamish are in demand as stage sets.

Rebuild

Buildings and landscapes do not stay the same forever. In fact styles can change quite dramatically and relatively quickly. In our own century, think of the changes that have occurred in house styles and interiors in each of the decades from the 1950s to the 1990s. Pure examples surviving from even these very recent times are almost impossible to find, hence the interest in reconstructions of modern room settings in museums such as the Castle Museum, York.

A shop interior at the North of England Open Air Museum, Beamish, County Durham.

Equally necessary may be the rebuilding of portions of buildings to enable their interpretation to take place. The facade of one of the buildings at the Weald and Downland Museum has had almost 90% of its timbers replaced, showing the fine line between restoration and reconstruction.

At other times a rebuild is more obvious and straightforward. Based upon as much historical data as possible, various buildings from the past have been reconstructed solely on archaeological and/or documentary evidence. Examples include the Lunt Roman fort at Baginton near Coventry, the Anglo-Saxon village at West Stow, Suffolk, and the Globe Theatre in Southwark, London.

Other rebuildings are brought about by disaster, such as fire or storm damage. A recent example of this would be the National Trust property of Uppark, on the South Downs near the Hampshire-Sussex border, where a fine late seventeenth century house was devastated by fire on 30 August 1989. The Trust took the bold decision to rebuild and restore all of the house together with a re-planning and re-planting of the garden at a total price of nearly £20 million. The rebuilding is not without controversy, with some arguing that the reconstruction pretends to be original when it is not. The view of the Trust is that a house like this lives on and that here was an opportunity for twentieth century craftsmen and women to use their skills and to relearn some of the skills of the seventeenth and eighteenth century that are required here and at other historic properties needing maintenance and repair.

The News, Portsmouth

Uppark, West Sussex, showing the devastation after fire swept through the National Trust property in 1989. The house has now been re-built and the interiors re-created.

Replicate

Replicas are most often associated with artefacts where a replica may be made for display or other interpretive reasons such as allowing visitors to handle objects and sometimes actually use them in the way in which they were designed to function. Other replicas may be made to sell so that the visitor can take away a link with the history of a site or building. If the intent is honest these are replicas, but if the intent is dishonest than the replica is a fake intended to fool or at the very least pretend to be something that it is not. Replicas may often be made with a telltale indication that they are replicas, for instance be stamped with the date of modern manufacture or be made of modern materials.

Occasionally replicas may be made of entire sites, or parts of a site. The most famous example of this is the Lascaux caves of France, where the original palaeolithic cave art was threatened by the atmospheric conditions created by visitors inside the caves. In order to preserve the cave art the genuine caves were shut, but in order to present this remarkable evidence to the public, a replica of part of Lascaux, known as Lascaux 2, was built near the original cave entrance and the cave art replicated.

Re-create

Sometimes the past is dealt with in another way, one that goes much further than reconstruction and is not a replica either. Whilst its core may be partly based on sound archaeological, ethnographical or documentary evidence (and may indeed use historic objects as in a museum tableau), it is enhanced by adding the ephemeral details of everyday life: the sort of details that can never be exactly as it was, but can represent the period, thus giving the re-creation a 'period feel'.

The rationale for such an approach is usually to enliven the scene, providing an enhanced insight into the way it might have been. This could include people in period dress acting the part (as at

BELOW: The Globe Theatre, London, under reconstruction.

BELOW: Saalburg Roman fort, Germany. After excavation in the nineteenth century, part of the fort was re-created in stone. This is the main entrance to the fort.

Richard Kalina/Shakespeare's Globe

Mike Corbishley

ABOVE: The Jorvik Viking Centre, York, has consistently been one of the most successful heritage attractions since it opened in 1983, with around 900,000 visitors per annum and a gross annual turnover of £2.5 million.

RIGHT: Williamsburg, Virginia, USA. From the 1920s this eighteenth-century town has been researched, excavated and then re-created as a living historical attraction. Williamsburg is now part of a protected area, the Colonial National Historical Park.

Colonial Williamsburg) or may have animated figures that do this (as at Jorvik Viking Centre, York). Proponents of this approach would argue that this intensifies an empathy for the past and encourages interest in the period being presented. There is also the entertainment value, which may well promote understanding and should certainly increase popularity.

Detractors of this approach would say that it places too much emphasis on entertaining and not enough on authenticity. With a commercial incentive to entertain, there may be a reluctance to present the negative aspects of the past, such as the squalor of Victorian slums, the dangers of working in a nineteenth century industry, or other issues perceived as difficult for the visitor. Some see this as the 'disneyfication' of the past, bringing too much of the superficiality of a Disneyland to the heritage. This is partly a misrepresentation of Disneyland, which does not set out to give an accurate history of the past: we all know that its purpose is to provide entertainment.

CAN IT EVER BE UNBIASED?

We have begun to discover that there is more than one way to interpret and present a heritage feature. Often the sheer volume of information available on certain aspects of the past will inevitably necessitate a selection being made. Conversely, other aspects will have little or no information or surviving evidence to allow them to be presented at all.

In other words the surviving sample of information is itself usually biased even before we face the very difficult task of deciding what to say or what not to say. Taken together with what we know about audience segmentation, the whole story is not only impossible to tell but also inappropriate given the limitation and variation of audience interest and ability. And of course there are always the constraints of limited space and frequently budgets. The result of all this will therefore be a selection, but one that should be built upon deliberate and explicit decisions about the content and its presentational form.

But there is still the difficult question of what and how much should be included and what should be excluded? There are two schools of

thought here. One would say that interpretation should strive to be unbiased, present the facts fairly and offer a balanced account of the heritage: for instance, in a country house, show what life was like for the servants, the cook, the chambermaids, and the gardeners as well as for the gentry, the squire, his family and friends. This approach would also promote openness about what we know or don't know about the past, describing, for example, alternative explanations for the development and use of certain archaeological sites, such as henges or causewayed enclosures, and leaving the visitor to make up his or her own mind.

The other school would start from the premise that most of the time we don't actually know what happened in the past, thus to describe unprovable statements as facts is misleading. It abandons the concept of 'truth' about the past and admits to a biased viewpoint from the outset. This form of presentation can be refreshingly alive and even exciting, discarding compromise to one side and putting in its place enthusiasm and boldness. An example of this approach could be seen at the Ulster Museum where the juxtaposition of orange and green cases presented the two traditions of the province.

LEFT: Avebury Museum, Wiltshire. Part of the museum displays created by English Heritage emphasise the limitations of archaeological evidence. The full-size Neolithic figure is presented in two halves: one shows the view of a fully dressed yet ragged individual. The other half is more 'sophisticated', painted and tattooed with well-made clothes and jewellery. (see Stone, 1994).

HOT INTERPRETATION

David Uzzell has drawn the distinction between a detached, objective and cool approach to presentation and one that is provoking, passionate and hot. He goes on to say that there are some issues involving personal values, beliefs and interests which will excite a degree of emotional arousal, even though they are contemplated in a calm and level headed way (Uzzell, 1989a, 34).

When dealing with sensitive issues such as the atrocities of war and man's inhumanity to man (religious persecution, ethnic cleansing) interpretation may try in vain to give an even handed treatment of the subject. This creates the danger of sanitising the image to make it less horrible, less shameful and more acceptable to an audience. Uzzell argues that this is a disservice to interpretation, with too much emphasis on the bland and not enough on the harsh reality of the past. He cites examples of interpretation at the Imperial War Museum that do not convey the awful conditions of life in the trenches in the First World War and the original omission in the English Heritage panel on Clifford's Tower in York of the massacre of 150 Jews who had taken refuge there in 1190.

There are two crucial points here. One is about perspective: whose view of the past is being presented? The other is about so-called objectivity: is there ever an objective view or just a consensus that holds sway at the present? Won't our views be re-interpreted in the years ahead? Why do we crave to present 'the truth' when truth will depend so much on viewpoint and the weighting of the very evidence that is presented or, indeed, omitted.

Heritage interpretation is not a soft option where all that is required is a nice, nostalgic view of the past. It requires a full working knowledge of the issues and the evidence, together with a willingness to be open about the strengths and weaknesses of our ability to interpret in a way that deepens the understanding of the visitor. If provocation is required to do that, then it should not be avoided for fear of presenting something upsetting.

MEASURING EFFECTIVENESS

The effectiveness of interpretation is determined by an objective assessment of how well it has performed its various functions, particularly those that were set out in its original aims and objectives. The evaluation of interpretation therefore starts with a re-examination of the aims and objectives that were established and agreed at the planning stage of the interpretation. These should set the criteria against which the success of the interpretation can be measured.

A generic set of criteria might include the following:

■ Has the intended audience visited the site?

■ Is the theme (or themes) of the interpretation obvious to the visitor?

■ Are the style and the methods used appropriate to the audience who have come?

Has the audience

■ enjoyed the interpretation?

■ understood the message?

■ learned something that they did not already know?

■ been emotionally moved by the interpretation?

■ been stimulated/provoked into some form of desired action?

■ Is the audience able to recall the main points of the interpretation: 5 minutes later? 1 hour later? 1 week later?

Most criteria may be commonly measured using 3 types of variables as defined by Shettel et al in a seminal work written in 1968 entitled *Strategies for Determining Exhibit Effectiveness*. These are:

■ Viewer variables: age, gender, socio-economic level, IQ, etc.

English Heritage

Exterior and an internal view of Clifford's Tower, York, showing the arrangements of interpretation panels which now include an account of the Jewish massacre there in 1190.

■ Design variables: length of text, its reading level and complexity, legibility, layout, use of graphics, use of interactives, audio-visuals, etc.

■ Exhibit effectiveness variables: the ability of the exhibit to attract the visitors' attention, to hold it, and bring about an increase in their interest and understanding; and, perhaps, to provoke the desired response.

All of the above can be measured in some way: some more easily than others. The most obvious way is by the use of surveys of one form or another, but these will have to be carefully devised and executed in order to obtain credible feedback.

At some point visitor numbers alone will be cited as a mark of success. Indeed some exhibitions are most memorable precisely because of the high visitor figures. Take for instance the so-called 'blockbuster' exhibitions like the 'Treasures of Tutankhamun' at the British Museum in 1972 (which attracted 1.6 million visitors) or 'The Genius of China' at the Royal Academy in 1973 (which attracted the record breaking daily attendance figure of 6,600). These exhibitions are in a league of their own attracting crowds partly because of the sense of occasion which offered a once in a lifetime opportunity to see unique and stunning collections.

But it is more than just numbers that matter, and some of the more interesting developments in evaluation have to do with assessing what people have learned. The context for carrying out such tests may well have to be wider than the heritage site itself. For instance, it may be useful to determine if people understand or appreciate an issue better having visited than those who haven't. This might involve setting a target: do people who visited understand 10%, 20% or 50% more than those who didn't?

Of course there are problems with assessment. Can understanding be accurately measured, especially from what may well be a biased sample in the first place? (the people who come may already know a great deal about the subject: that could be why they are there!). This is an instance where previously collected data on visitors, (eg their pre-knowledge of the subject) becomes vitally important at the assessment stage.

We have already seen how difficult it is to determine whether presenting the past is ever objective or not. Likewise it is difficult to know if there is a truly objective test for the effectiveness of interpretation. Designers themselves have been unsure about this for some time (Hall, 1987,116), but for our purposes it is important to realise that interpretation must be able to explain and justify itself by providing evidence that it is up to the job.

PRACTICAL FEEDBACK

Upon completion, interpretation will need to be evaluated for more prosaic reasons. For instance does it work practically? Is there sufficient space for visitors, including disabled visitors, to circulate? Is information supplied in the right places and at the right height? Does the writing style help the interpretation or only get in the way? Are the display materials appropriate in style and are they standing up to the job? Of course all these factors should have been adequately and effectively considered at the planning and development stages, but they will need to be re-assessed in the harsh light of reality and where the views of the customers are listened to.

As well as meeting other targets, the funding organisation will need to know that they have achieved value for money. If improvements are required, what do they need to spend more money on and why.

Interpretation must also be evaluated for another practical reason. Once created it does not maintain itself in perfect order. Displays will begin to look dated or even worn out and will need attention. While obvious, this is an area where many heritage venues, including museums, let themselves down. Money for maintenance is not always as forthcoming as money for glamorous new presentations. Like most products, exhibitions have a certain 'shelf-life' and need to be designed and produced with a specific life-expectancy in mind. This is yet another variable that will need to be clearly expressed at the outset and taken into account at all stages of development, production and assessment.

LEFT: An adult education group discuss the recently-produced (1978) interpretation for part of the Roman remains in Lincoln.

ABOVE: Fishbourne Roman Palace, West Sussex. Minimalist interpretation (in 1983) does not interfere with the excavated and displayed ruins.

LEFT: A traditional interpretation on the streets of York. How well does it do its job of imparting information?

CONFLICTS IN THE HERITAGE

IDENTIFYING AND RESOLVING CONFLICTS

The site of Fountains Abbey and Studley Royal Park in Yorkshire is one of the most remarkable in Europe, encompassing the spectacular ruins of a twelfth century Cistercian Abbey, a Jacobean mansion, one of the best surviving examples of a Georgian green water garden, and a nineteenth century church built by William Burges. Lakes, avenues, temples, ruins and cascades combine to provide a built landscape within a remote environment of incredible beauty and tranquillity. In recognition of its importance and uniqueness, it has been designated by UNESCO as a World Heritage Site.

The majority of this site, 400 acres of it, is preserved and managed by the National Trust, in fact it is the Trust's most visited property. It is the firmly held belief within the Trust that visitors can only fully appreciate the site's beauty if they understand something of the Cistercian order, with its emphasis on austerity and the need for isolation in a wild environment (Waterson, 1989).

The potential for conflict is obvious and is an exceedingly common one at historic and natural sites, namely how to provide the necessary facilities for interpretation together with the other requirements that large numbers of visitors require such as toilets and restaurants, without spoiling a part of the site itself. In the end, and after much deliberation, a new visitor reception building was located on a site near the Abbey, but carefully sited so as not intrude into the beauty and austerity of the Cistercian setting.

This is a growing problem for successful ('success', that is, measured in visitor numbers) organisations like the National Trust where the conflict between preservation

and presentation is constantly present. After all, the Trust's original principles when founded in 1895 were not concerned wholly with preservation, but also with allowing people to come and enjoy natural and historic sites. This it has done so successfully that it is now asking the question 'are there too many visitors?' (Stirling, 1990,).

Interpretation has an important role to play here. First, by pointing out the problem to the visitors themselves and increasing their awareness of the issues. Second, where space allows, interpretation centres should be located away from the main focus of visitor attention, helping to spread the load over the entire site. This can allow for car parks to be set further away provided some form of disabled visitor access is maintained. 'Spreading the load' is an important marketing concept too, attempting to get the visitors to change their visiting plans and come 'out of season' or, even better, tempt them to go somewhere else completely, preferably somewhere less intensively visited and more able to take the strain.

Of course this does not solve the problem in the longer term, and many sites that have been promoted in this way are now themselves reaching saturation point. The Yorkshire Moors National Park was partly promoted to take the strain off the Lake District, but has now itself reached 11 million visitors a year and the numbers are still rising.

WHOSE PAST IS IT ANYWAY?

Throughout this part of the book, we have been examining ways of interpreting and presenting the past to a variety of different audiences. This still leaves two fundamental and often controversial questions unresolved, namely with whose past are we dealing (or not dealing) and to whom are we presenting it (or not presenting it)?

There are certain parts of the past which are either seldom preserved or seldom the subject of presentation. The heritage of minority groups has perhaps suffered the most from this over the years. For instance, until very recently, there were few museum displays about aspects of the heritage of non-western Europeans despite the fact that Britain is a multicultural society today. Or there may be historical issues that have not been the subject of adequate interpretation, such as the slave trade and slavery in the eighteenth and nineteenth centuries (for a recent attempt at displaying this subject refer to the Merseyside Maritime Museum's

The visitor reception building at Fountains Abbey, North Yorkshire.

Mark Brisbane

exhibition entitled Transatlantic Slavery: Against Human Dignity, reviewed by Devenish, 1995).

Presentation is inextricably linked to what is known about a person or group of people, a place or an event. If adequate documentation and artefactual evidence does not survive than it will be difficult to treat the subject in any depth. But if museums and other places associated with preserving the past, collect only that evidence that is associated with the status quo, then how will other groups ever be able to appear? If a local museum does not collect evidence on the issues that have concerned and indeed influenced the local population, then what hope of presenting topics that are connected to today's local inhabitants. Or if the donors of collections are always from the same socio-economic or political background, then obviously displays will be heavily weighted in favour of these collections both now and in the future.

Gender issues

Susan Pearce (1993) raised this last point in connection with male and female collections, posing the question 'where are the female collectors?'. She argues that women not only collect in a different manner from men, working within the web of personal relationships and not within a perceived intellectual tradition, but also that the style of the collection is quite different.

Collections by men are often accompanied by the accoutrements of collecting such as special equipment, display cabinets and even the museum building itself and the collection is organised in a formal, systematic and scientific way. The female collection, often in a domestic setting, has meaning taken from personal and emotional relationships and may therefore be judged as 'not appropriate' (by both the potential donor and the recipient) as a 'serious' contender for preservation.

Political issues

Another case where interpretation is almost impossible occurs when a dominant group has excluded, through political and social controls, other sections of society from having any history at all. Distorting the past for political ends is not new, and the Third Reich certainly knew of its great propaganda value

Mike Corbishley

Visitors to the Elgin Marbles at the British Museum, London.

in spreading their views on so-called Aryan supremacy. Recent examples of this form of distortion would include South Africa where under apartheid the black majority where written out of history. Text books, schools, the media, and museums distorted and ignored the story of their past. A recognition of the importance of restoring the material culture and historical documentation of the non-white peoples of South Africa is now established, with the creation of centres for archives and cultural objects, especially those concerned with the recent past. This has led to a re-assessment of the collecting policies of the South African Museum. These issues are dealt with in detail in *The Presented Past* (Stone and Molyneux, 1994).

Views on the ownership of the past create problems in other ways which impact on interpretation. For instance, should the Elgin Marbles held by the British Museum since 1816, be returned to Athens so that they can be presented in, or at least near, their original setting? The Greeks (and many others) feel they should, especially as the Greeks never agreed to their removal. If a return is valid for the Marbles, why not for many other objects which were taken from their original setting but are now held in national museums around the world?

And are there topics that just should not be addressed at all: taboo issues that, although they are

part of mankind's heritage, are outside the boundaries of 'good taste' or 'decent society'. War is part of that heritage, but how much gore and horror should or shouldn't be included? Why or why not? And what about patriotism? When does it become jingoism and nationalistic zenophobia and how should we deal with this when it has appeared in the past? Sex, disease and death are also difficult topics to interpret. Does this mean that we shouldn't?

Access to the heritage

Finally to return to the audience, for whom, at least in theory, all this presentation is supposed to exist. We have referred to groups who have been excluded from the historical record and are therefore precluded from appearing in subsequent interpretation, but there are also those who may well be excluded from visiting for direct or indirect reasons. The former could include those for whom physical barriers make it impossible or extremely difficult to obtain access: a lack of suitable surfaces for disabled visitors or no facilities for families with pushchairs. Visually impaired people may feel excluded unless some careful thought has been put into presentations that are accessible for them such as tactile experiences, audio facilities, or large print (there are approximately 1 million people registered blind or partially sighted in the UK: about

Great Zimbabwe, Zimbabwe. The conical tower inside the Great Enclosure. This is a World Heritage Site, despite years of misinterpretation by the white regime.

65% of visually impaired people can read large print).

While the reading level of text will generally be set for an intended audience, what about those who require either more or different information or information presented in another manner to make the interpretation useful to them? This would include visitors with special needs or with difficulty reading. For those with learning difficulties clear labels and signs, use of large print and specially tailored taped tours may all be appropriate.

The issue of widening access is one that is now familiar to curators, interpreters and others involved in designing and marketing exhibitions, attractions, etc. They are now well aware of the need to open up interpretation for the many differing requirements of the audience (McGinnis, 1994) and recognize that the best way to improve the situation is to consult with groups of disabled people from the planning stage right through to the evaluation of the finished product.

People may also be excluded by financial factors, such as the cost of getting to a venue or site, or by the price of admission, or both. The debate on charging for access to the heritage, especially museum admissions, is one which has waxed and waned for more than twenty years. Should there be free access to the heritage? Don't most people already contribute to the maintenance of certain venues (eg publicly run museums) through taxation?

Most venues have avoided at least part of the argument against charging by setting concessionary rates. Some have free days, free events, or times when they are free for local residents. Many do not charge for pre-booked school parties, but this is changing rapidly with local authority run sites and museums having to introduce charges even for this category of visit. In 1995 Bristol City Museum and Art Gallery reluctantly agreed to extend charging to all schools using the education service and the school loans service, owing to cuts by the soon to be abolished Avon County Council.

The figures would certainly seem to indicate that charging does directly effect visitor numbers. When Winchester City Museum removed their charges in 1986 the number of visitors doubled from just under 20,000 to just over 40,000 per annum. The same effect is evident for other venues that removed charges in the mid-1980s such as Birmingham Nature Centre, the Museum of Oxford, Moyse's Hall in Bury St Edmunds and the London Transport Museum. Visits in 1992 to the top 20 free museums went up by 5%, while the top 20 charging museums saw their number of visitors drop by 1% (Davies, 1994, 75).

While most visitors say that they are willing to pay a 'reasonable fee' for admissions, non-frequent visitors are less prepared to pay. In visitor surveys carried out by a number of national museums in England and Wales, the largest decline in visitor numbers due to charging was noted in the following groups; casual visitors, those on short visits, those with children, regular visitors, those in lower income groups and the under 20s: in other words the very groups that most museums would like to attract in order to extend their audience and reach a representative cross section of the population (figures cited in Davies, 1994, 75). This serves to underline the complexity of the idea of freedom of access to interpretation: not only does the audience need to be there, but once there individual visitors need to feel included, not alienated, by what is going on.

CURRENT ISSUES

The concept of heritage and its myriad components is so wide ranging that it embraces almost all modern day controversies from global, life or death issues, such as ethnic cleansing and the destruction of cultural heritage in Bosnia, to locally significant ones, such as the felling of trees planted in commemoration of Canadian soldiers who fought in the Second World War to make way for road improvements. This section will examine a few of the heritage-related debates that are currently making the news.

Ethnicity

We all have ethnic affiliations, but within most countries and cultures there tend to be certain groups which dominate by virtue of their economic and social position. The history and heritage that receives the most attention (and most expenditure) is most often that which is valued by these people.

In recent years, however, there has been a growing demand coming from minority groups who share their own common experiences, perhaps also a common homeland or a particularly distinctive material culture, to have an equal, or at least some, recognition of the needs of their history and culture.

In certain circumstances it is extremely difficult for one group to agree to the rights of another to preserve and promote their heritage. This is most obvious in the case of war, when the rights of one group are not only denied but obliterated by an opposing group. The recent war in the former Yugoslavia is the worst, recent example. Starting in 1991, it was not enough for the invaders to 'cleanse' the local population, they also tried to remove all traces of the population's presence. Cultural monuments were deliberately targeted, especially those that were of symbolic (and national) value. This war, like so many before it, has seen a great deal of destruction aimed at churches, mosques, villages, mansions, and museums. Shelling the historic town of Dubrovnik, for instance, had no military justification, but was done as an anti-cultural act to demoralize the enemy.

While the excesses of war produce the most intense cases of cul-

Mike Corbishley

tural domination and destruction, there are other examples, including the manipulation of the archaeological evidence in the former Rhodesia where the white regime suppressed the evidence about the site of Great Zimbabwe, to ensure that it was not publicly acknowledged that it had been built by the indigenous black population.

Another case is that of the acquisition and display of Australian Aboriginal and Native American skeletal remains and sacred objects collected by ninteenth and twentieth century archaeologists and anthropologists. Some of these collections have been used for research and study in Western museums and arguments for their retention by the museums were put forward for many years. Recently however, the demands for their return have begun to be acknowledged and collections, particularly of skeletal remains, are being returned for re-burial. The World Archaeological Congress (WAC) has been instrumental in promoting the rights of native populations to gain access to their heritage and to obtain the repatriation of their ancestors. In 1989 WAC published a Code of Practice for archaeologists on the subject of the treatment, reburial and repatriation of human remains, known as the Vermillion Accord, which was drafted in conjunction with representatives from native populations.

A rather different case concerns the preservation of contentious reminders of people's inhumanity to each other. Should the Nazi concentration camps be preserved and if so how should they be pre-

sented: as memorials or museums? Auschwitz has been designated a World Heritage Site: does this imply it should be kept as a monument to collective national guilt or to reconciliation?

On a more general level, ethnic groups are increasing their demands for access to their heritage, for an equal opportunity to collect and to display their past. Heritage sites and museums will have to continue to develop ways of meeting these demands.

The antiquities trade

The trade in cultural property is big business. Heritage does not only have a cultural value, but also a monetary value and therefore people can buy and sell parts of it in the market place. Unfortunately, due partly to its very nature and, ironically, to its 'protection' through legislation, it is also very likely to be bought and sold on the black market.

The size of the trade in illegally obtained cultural property is enormous. Most of it derives from robbed archaeological sites and theft of art objects from institutions and private collections. It has recently been estimated that almost 95% of all known archaeological sites in Costa Rica have been plundered. In India, between 1977 and 1979, there were 3,000 thefts of antiquities reported, yet only 10 cases were solved (Greenfield, 1989, 239). In Italy where the theft of antiquities from sites has been a problem for many years, there is a specialist police force known as the Commando Carabinieri Tutela Patrimino Artistico, which was set

up to protect the country's heritage.

Despite these measures and tough legislation on the export of antiquities in many countries, such as Turkey and Egypt, the enforcement of these laws is very difficult indeed as the financial incentive to carry out illegal trade is so great. The situation is not helped by the many variations in national laws in this complex area; and of course, these laws are very dependent on international cooperation and policing, the latter largely through the International Criminal Police Organization (Interpol). Interpol, indeed, has a special unit to deal with stolen art and heritage objects, which sends out circulars to relevant agencies, national police forces and customs authorities.

The auction houses and art sales rooms of the USA, Germany, Switzerland, France, England and Hong Kong are the most common destinations for much of this illicitly obtained material. In Switzerland there is no restriction on the import or export of works of art and cultural heritage, making it a leading centre for the sale of stolen material, especially from Italy, Greece, Turkey, Tunisia and Egypt. The United States is one of only a handful of countries without any export regulations for cultural property and their auction houses are regulated, if at all, by different laws in different states.

In 1970 UNESCO drafted a convention on the means of prohibiting and preventing the illicit import, export and transfer of ownership of cultural property. For the purposes of this convention 'cultural property' was defined as including any item which the member state had designated as being important, on secular or religious grounds, for archaeology, prehistory, history, literature, art or science. Article 1 of the convention went on to identify categories which could be included. These were the following: fauna, flora, minerals and anatomy; property relating to history; archaeological discoveries; elements of monuments; antiquities (more than 100 years old); ethnological items; pictures, paintings, drawings, statuary, engravings, prints and lithographs; manuscripts

Dachau Concentration Camp is now classified in Germany as a memorial site and is open to the public.

and books; postage stamps; archives; and furniture and musical instruments (more than 100 years old).

The Convention was enacted in April 1972 and by 1993 almost 70 countries had signed the Convention thereby becoming parties to it. However, as of the end of 1995, the UK government had still not become a signatory, preferring to rely upon voluntary codes of practice written, endorsed and applied by the art trade itself. These codes are similar to those already adopted by the museums' profession in the UK, which in its *Code of Practice for Museum Authorities* states quite clearly that it accepts the principles set out in the UNESCO Convention and goes on to state that museums and galleries in the UK 'do not and will not willingly acquire any antiquities or other cultural material which they have reason to believe has been exported in contravention of the current laws of the country of origin'.

Along with the problem of the trade in illicitly obtained material is the related issue of retaining cultural property in its country of origin rather than allowing it to be legally sold abroad. In the UK the decision to restrict export is taken on the merits of each case as it arises. It is first brought before the Export Reviewing Committee on Works of Art, which make a recommendation to the Secretary of State for Trade and Industry. If the Secretary of State decides it should be 'saved for the nation' he issues a temporary ban on its export. This ban will remain in force for a limited time while the purchase price is raised by one or more appropriate institution (usually a national museum). The government may assist with the purchase by supporting an appeal for funds by the museum with grant aid.

Finally, whether legally or illegally traded, the movement of cultural property away from its place of origin, destroying, possibly forever, the link with its historical context, is an extremely serious issue and one which appears to be receiving increasing media attention. Unfortunately, however, during the 25 years since the UNESCO Convention was first promulgated, there has been little real progress in curtailing illegal activities associated with obtaining and dealing in

Mike Corbishley

The Roman Forum, Rome. Visitors throng the site all year round.

this area, which is still the second largest illegal trade after drugs.

Tourism impacts worldwide

We have already touched on the relationship between tourism and heritage and seen that tourism has both positive and negative impacts. As tourism is predicted to grow still further, assessing and ameliorating these impacts is a very vital issue for both the developed and the developing world.

The World Tourism Organisation forecasts a doubling of the numbers travelling from 300 million in 1990 to 600 million by the year 2000. And countries such as India, Kenya, Mexico, South Africa and Thailand are expecting to see tourism become increasingly important to them economically.

Angus Stirling, until recently the Director-General of the National Trust, has written about the need to develop strategies that not only respect but also reinforce three essential components of tourism, namely

■ the enjoyment and recreation of the visitor;

■ the conservation of indigenous life, beauty and the character of the place visited;

■ and the maximum economic return consistent with the first two.

He also recognized that tourism is a global issue, no one country can resolve the problem of too many visitors on its own. Furthermore, a

policy for tourism needs to address the situation at international, national, regional and local level. To do this it must have an overall set of principles that can be applied consistently. Sterling (1990) went on to suggest some proposals for a Code of Practice that faced up to these issues. It included the following:

■ Comprehensive tourist development plans are essential as the precondition for developing any tourist potential.

■ It should be a fundamental principle of any tourist development plan that both conservation, in its widest sense, and tourism benefit from it. This principle should be part of the constitutional purpose of all national tourist agencies, and of local authority tourism and recreation departments.

■ A significant proportion of revenue earned from tourism should be applied for the benefit of conservation, both nationally and regionally.

■ The best long-term interests of the people living and working in any host community should be the primary determining factor in selecting options for tourist development.

■ Educational programmes should assist and invite tourists to respect

tourism policy and should take these factors into account.

■ The design of buildings, sites, and transport systems should minimize the potentially harmful visual effects of tourism. Pollution controls should be built in to all forms of infrastructure. Where sites of great natural beauty are concerned, the intrusion of built structures should be avoided if possible.

■ Good management should define the level of acceptable tourism development and provide controls to maintain that level.

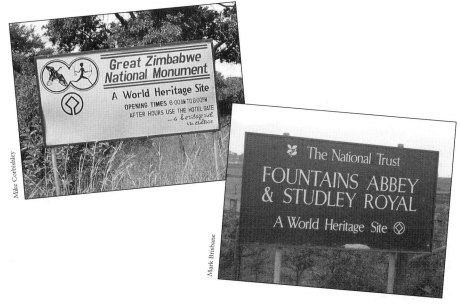

DEVELOPING INTEGRATED APPROACHES

In 1972 UNESCO promulgated the Convention Concerning the Protection of the World Cultural and Natural Heritage. This established the concept of World Heritage Sites, set up a World Heritage Committee and a World Heritage Fund. As with all UNESCO conventions, member states must individually adopt and ratify them before they can come into force. In 1973 the United States was the first country to ratify the World Heritage Convention, the UK doing so in 1984. By 1991 120 countries had ratified the convention, and by this time 337 properties from 73 different member states had been accepted onto the World Heritage List. These comprised 245 cultural sites, 78 natural sites and 14 a mixture of the two.

The general criteria for allowing sites to go forward for designation as World Heritage Sites are as follows:

■ They must be of outstanding universal value

■ Overall, a balance between cultural and natural heritage is attempted, but there is no set limit or number per country

■ There is a prerequisite prior to submission to the World Heritage Committee that an inventory must be produced of all sites which a member state is intending to submit over the next 5 - 10 years

■ 'Buffer zones' around each pro-

posed site should be stipulated with details on its use, size and characteristics

■ An action plan should be submitted for each site especially where the site is threatened by "the action of man".

Once designated, there is a limited amount of financial assistance, predominantly available to third world countries, through UNESCO's World Heritage Fund. The Fund was established in 1976 and will contribute towards:

■ the cost of preparing submission

■ emergency assistance to World Heritage Sites for a genuine crisis

■ training for conservators, architects and other specialists

■ promotional activities.

In the UK, sites are listed by the Department of National Heritage and nominated by them to the World Heritage Committee.

The benefits of World Heritage Site designation are rather illusive. On the positive side, they raise the awareness and profile of heritage on to a world stage and allow developing countries to receive limited support for conserving and presenting their premiere sites. In England, Planning Policy Guidance 15, paragraph 2.22 states that inclusion highlights the outstanding international importance of designated Sites as *a key material consideration* 'to be taken

into account by local planning authorities in determining planning and listed building consent applications, and by the Secretary of State in determining cases on appeal or following call-in'. PPG 15 goes on to state that each local authority concerned with a World Heritage Site should formulate specific planning policies for its protection and should include these policies in their development plans. Significant development proposals affecting World Heritage Sites will generally require formal environmental assessment, to ensure that their immediate impact and their implications for the longer term are fully evaluated (PPG 15, paragraph 2.23).

Nevertheless, despite this limited acknowledgement that World Heritage Sites require some extra protection, there are problems associated with designation. These may include for certain sites the added pressure on them from overvisiting, precisely due to their perceived higher status amongst tourists. In the UK this problem has been identified at Bath and Fountains Abbey.

There is no special responsibility for World Heritage Sites at the national or local level - sites gain no further specific protection from designation (in the UK, sites must rely on existing procedures such as planning legislation, listed building and scheduled ancient monument protection, etc). There is also a lack of consultation between those who designate and those who conserve and manage the individual sites. Most experts agree that there is an urgent need to develop effec-

English Heritage

LEFT: Hebden Bridge, Calderdale. A conservation area scheme established in 1987-88 in which grants provided jointly by English Heritage and the local authority were put towards the repair of specific buildings in the town.

tive monitoring and management strategies for these sites.

One of the non-governmental organisations that has been pressing for these and other improvements in the UNESCO Convention, as well as monitoring the impact of tourism on World Heritage and other sites, is the International Council of Monuments and Sites, (ICOMOS), which was established out of the Second International Congress of Architects held in Venice in 1964.

National links: statements of intent

Different heritage organisations may have opposing views on what is best for the preservation of the heritage. For instance, what is appropriate for the well-being of wildlife or flora may be detrimental to the very survival of archaeological remains. In order to achieve their aims and at the same time protect the best interests of the environment, a number of organisations have agreed statements of intent which set out clearly and succinctly how they will work together and communicate with one another.

Two recent examples of agreed statements are between English Nature and English Heritage, and Scottish Natural Heritage and Historic Scotland. These have included agreeing a number of common goals, such as improving the management of the natural heritage through a better understanding of the archaeological and historical record; and of the archaeological and historical record through a fuller appreciation of its setting and of the natural resources which provide for, and limit, human activity. The SNH/HS statement of intent goes on to say that they will endeavour to avoid damage to, and where appropriate to improve the condition of, archaeological and historical features as a result of management actions designed to maintain natural heritage interests. Likewise, they will also endeavour to conserve, and where appropriate enhance, the natural heritage interest of sites and areas of archaeological and historical significance.

These common goals can be achieved through liaison on policy matters, consultation over the designation of protected areas, and establishing procedures to ensure that the implementation of their respective policies do not conflict. For instance, SNH and HS have agreed to develop management techniques and consultation procedures to achieve maximum mutual benefit from any management plans prepared on behalf of each organisation and to liaise when grant aiding management works to ensure that their respective interests are considered.

There is also the public presentation side to these cooperative agreements, where organisations undertake to work together on certain interpretative projects, on developing and delivering educational policy, and producing joint publications.

Of course, these documents will need to be more than a collection of fine words. The test must come in the form of results, preferably results that can be measured in the number of successful collaborations, environmental enhancements, and facilities and opportunities for the public to enjoy and appreciate the heritage, both natural and cultural. Nevertheless, the beginning of a more open and cooperative phase of working practices between different organisations and professionals must be an important and potentially very beneficial development.

Local authorities and local links

Despite the changing structure and role of local government it still has a key part to play in enabling heritage issues to be raised and dealt with by encouraging conservation initiatives and facilitating their implementation. Local authorities (old and new, unitary and non-unitary) will continue to have a critical role in the protection and enhancement of the heritage. For instance, the Department of National Heritage has recently asked new authorities to ensure that there is adequate provision for maintaining SMR and Historic Building Records, as well as continuing to ensure their commitment to heritage conservation through planning and development control. This includes ensuring that development plans adequately reflect the conservation needs of the area and that they have access to all fields of conservation advice (Guidance Note for New Authorities, DNH, August 1995)

Of course, local authorities recognise that conservation makes an important contribution to local economic prosperity by encouraging the growth of tourism and by providing an attractive living and working environment that promotes inward investment to an area. Conservation staff within authorities provide a vital service by contributing to strategic regeneration initiatives, conservation area designation, building repair and re-use proposals and grant-aid schemes.

Local authorities have a statutory duty to preserve or enhance the character or appearance of conservation areas, of which there are now over 8,000 in England alone. Grants offered under the new English Heritage conservation area partnership scheme (CAPS) will introduce greater delegation of management to local authorities and an enhanced role for their conservation staff. While their ability to fund projects may have decreased somewhat in recent years they still are a significant contributor and can be vital in the early days of a project to provide start up support and 'pump priming' resources.

As importantly as funding they provide a framework, sometimes through enforcing national legislation, for the planning process, for advice to voluntary organisations and individuals, and educating the public about their environment. They also provide support for non-statutory undertakings such as museums and galleries - the majority of museums in the UK are under local authority control - and are therefore responsible directly for the care and presentation of extremely important local and national collections.

Local authorities also have an interest in historic properties and sites, some of which are under direct council ownership and control, such as the Great Hall, Winchester owned and managed by Hampshire County Council. Others may be owned by the council, but managed by some other organisation. An example is the Medieval Merchant's House in Southampton, owned by the City Council, but under the guardianship of English Heritage who restored it and now manage its presentation to the public.

Local authorities are also especially important in the role they play in the increasing use of management agreements with private landowners where principles of land management are agreed, taking into account the needs of archaeological and ecological sites, plants and animals, and the preservation of particular land use patterns and historic landscapes.

A notable example of integrated conservation management is the Somerset Levels and Moors Project which was initiated under the auspices of Somerset County Council in 1991. The project was funded by the Council with support from the Countryside Commission and English Heritage. Two project officers were employed to promote the conservation of the Somerset Levels and Moors; one a wetland ecologist, the other an archaeologist. This duality of experience and expertise was then brought to bear on the issues of strategic policy and planning for the area, planning and development control and the establishment of visitor facilities, interpretation and education material.

The Somerset project has achieved a considerable measure of success in forging links and common goals between the disparate conservation interests and agencies working in the area. It has also managed to integrate successfully archaeological and landscape concerns into the overall conservation agenda for the area.

ABOVE: Medieval Merchant's House, Southampton.

LEFT: Hadrian's Wall, Northumbria, a World Heritage Site, where the designation helped to stop proposals for potentially damaging development.

BIBLIOGRAPHY

Aldous, T, **New shopping in historic towns: the Chesterfield story**, English Heritage, 1990, ISBN 1-85074-298-7. ⋆

Alexander, E P, **Museums in Motion: An Introduction to the History and Functions of Museums**, American Association for State and Local History, 1979, ISBN 0-910050-35-X.

Apted, M, Gilyard Beer, R and Saunders, A D, **Ancient Monuments and their Interpretation**, Phillimore, 1977, ISBN 0-85033-239-7.

Baker, D B, **Living with the Past: The Historic Environment**, D Baker, 1983, ISBN 0-9508681-1-6.

Baker, F and Thomas, J (eds), **Writing the Past in the Present**, Saint David's University College, Lampeter, 1990, ISBN 0-905285-25.

Belcher, M, **Exhibitions in Museums**, Leicester University Press, 1991, ISBN 0-7185-1299-5.

Binford, L R, **In Pursuit of the Past**, Thames and Hudson, 1983, ISBN 0-500-27494-0.

Binks, G et al, **Visitors Welcome: A manual on the presentation and interpretation of archaeological excavations**, 1988, English Heritage, ISBN 0-11-701210-6.⋆

Bintliff, J (ed), **Extracting Meaning from the Past**, Oxbow Books, 1988, ISBN 0-946897-16-6.

Brooks, C, **The Albert Memorial**, English Heritage, 1995, ISBN 1-85074-600-1.⋆

Chamberlin, E R, **Preserving the Past**, Dent, 1979, ISBN 0-460-04364-1.

Chippindale, C et al, **Who Owns Stonehenge?**, Batsford, 1990, ISBN 0-7134-6455-0.

Christian, R, **Vanishing Britain**, David and Charles, 1977, ISBN 0-715-37346-3.

Cleal, R M J, Walker, K E and Montague, R, **Stonehenge in its Landscape: Twentieth-century excavations**, English Heritage, 1995, ISBN 1-85074-605-2.⋆

Cleere, H (ed), **Approaches to the Archaeological Heritage**, Cambridge University Press, 1984, ISBN 0521-24305-X.

Cleere, H (ed), **Archaeological Heritage Management in the Modern World**, Routledge, 1989, ISBN 004-445028-1.

Conservation in London: A study of strategic planning policy in London, English Heritage/London Planning Advisory Committee, 1995, ISBN 1-85074-522-6. ⋆

Corbishley, M and Stone P G, 'The teaching of the past in formal school curricula in England' in **The Presented Past**, Stone, P G and Molyneaux, B L (eds), 1994, p 383-397.

Cormack, P, **Heritage in Danger**, New English Library, 1976, ISBN 0-450-03060-1.

Daniel, G and Renfrew, C, **The Idea of Prehistory**, Edinburgh University Press, 1988, ISBN 0-85224-536-X.

Darley, G, **Villages of Vision**, Architectural Press, 1975, ISBN 85139-707-0.

Darvill, T, **Ancient Monuments in the Countryside: an archaeological management review**, English Heritage, 1987, ISBN 1-85074-167-0. ⋆

Davies, S, **By Popular Demand: A strategic analysis of the market potential for museums and art galleries in the UK**, Museums and Galleries Commission, 1994, ISBN 0-948-63030-2.

Dean, D, **Museum Exhibition: Theory and Practice**, Routledge, 1994, ISBN 0-415-08016-9.

Devenish, D C, **Slavery: in the grip of prejudice?** in Museums Journal, vol 95, no 3, March 1995, p 20-1, ISSN 0-027-416-X.

Erder, C, **Our Architectural Heritage: from consciousness to conservation**, UNESCO/HMSO, 1989, ISBN 92-3-102363-2.

Fladmark, J M (ed), **Heritage: Conservation, Interpretation, and Enterprise**, Donhead Publishing, 1993, ISBN 1-873394-13-6.

Fladmark, J M (ed), **Cultural Tourism**, Donhead Publishing, 1994, ISBN 1-873394-15-2.

Fladmark, J M, **The Wealth of a Nation: Heritage as a cultural and competitive asset**, Robert Gordon University, Aberdeen, 1994, ISBN 0-9506289-3-X.

Fowler, P J, 'The Contemporary Past' in **Landscape and Culture: geographical and archaeological perspectives**, J M Wagstaff (ed), p 173-191, Blackwell, 1987, ISBN 0-631-13729-7.

Fowler, P J, **The Past in Contemporary Society: Then, Now**, Routledge, 1992, ISBN 0-415-06726-X.

Gathercole, P and Lowenthal, D (eds), **The Politics of the Past**, Routledge, 1990, ISBN 0-04-445018-4.

Greenfield, J, **The Return of Cultural Treasures**, Cambridge University Press, 1990, ISBN 0-521-33319-9.

Hall, M, **On Display**, Lund Humphries, 1987, ISBN 0-85331-455-1.

Harrison, R(ed), **Manual of Heritage Management**, Butterworth-Heinemann/ Association of Independent Museums, 1994, ISBN 0-7506-0822-6.

Hewison, R, **The Heritage Industry: Britain in a climate of decline**, Methuen, 1987, ISBN 0-413-16110-2.

Hodder, I, 'Changing Configurations: the relationship between theory and practice' in **Archaeological Resource Management in the UK: an Introduction**, J Hunter and I Ralston (eds), p 11-18.

Hood, M G, 'Staying Away: Why people choose not to visit museums', Museum News 61, 4 (April 1983), p 50-7.

Hughes, M and Rowley, T (eds), **The Management and Presentation of Field Monuments**, Department of External Studies, University of Oxford, 1986, ISBN 0-903736-21-7.

Hunter, J and Ralston I, (eds), **Archaeological Resource Management in the UK: an Introduction**, Alan Sutton/Institute of Field Archaeologists, 1993, ISBN 0-7509-0275-2.

Issues: urban areas - growth and change, Hobsons/English Heritage/Commission for the New Towns, 1994, ISBN 1-85324-990-4. ⋆

Johnstone, C and Weston W, **The Which? Heritage Guide**, 1981.

Kavanagh, G (ed), **Museum Languages**, Leicester University Press, 1991, ISBN 0-7185-1359-2.

Lavery, P and Cooper, C, **Planning and conservation - a case study of Maiden Castle**, Longman, 1988, ISBN 1-582-17356-6. ★

Layton, R (ed), **Who needs the Past? Indigenous Values and Archaeology**, Routledge, 1988, ISBN 0-04-445020-6.

Lipe, W D, **'Value and meaning in cultural resources'** in **Approaches to the Archaeological Heritage**, Cleere, H (ed), p 1-11.

Lowenthal, D, **The Past is a Foreign Country**, Cambridge University Press, 1985, ISBN 0-521-29480-0.

Lowenthal, D and Binney, M (eds), **Our Past Before Us - Why do we save it?**, Temple Smith, 1981, ISBN 0-85117-219-9.

Lumley, R, **The Museum Time-Machine**, Routledge, 1988, ISBN 0-415-00652-X.

MacEwen A and M, **National Parks - Conservation or Cosmetics?**, Allen and Unwin, 1982, ISBN 0-04-719004-3.

MacInnes, L, and Wickham-Jones, C R, **All Natural Things: Archaeology and the green debate**, Oxbow, 1992, ISBN 0-946897-45-X.

McGinnis, R, **'The Disabling Society'**, in Museums Journal, vol 94, no 6, June 1994, p 27-33, ISSN 0-027-416-X.

McManus, P M, **'Making Sense of Exhibits'** in **Museum Languages**, G Kavanagh (ed),1991, p 35-46.

Meyer, K, **The Plundered Past**, Atheneum Press, 1973, ISBN 0-241-02448-X.

Miles, R S et al, **The Design of Educational Exhibits**, Unwin Hyman, 1988, 2nd Edition, ISBN 0-04-069002-4.

Newcomb, R M, **Planning the Past**, Dawson, 1979, ISBN 0-7129-0816-1.

Palmer, M and Neaverson, P (eds), **Managing the Industrial Heritage**, Leicester University Press, 1995, ISBN 0-9510377-5-7.

Pearce, D, **Conservation Today**, Routledge, 1989, ISBN 0-415-03914-2.

Pearce, S, **'Making Up is Hard To Do'**, in Museums Journal, vol 93, no 12, December 1993, p 25-27, ISSN 0-027-416-X.

Renfrew, C and Bahn, P, **Archaeology: theories, methods and practice**, Thames and Hudson, 1991, ISBN 0-500-27605-6.

Rumble, P, **'Interpreting the Built and Historic Environment'** in Heritage Interpretation, Uzzell D (ed), 1989, p 24-32.

Saint, A, **A change of heart - English architecture since the war**, Royal Commission on the Historical Monuments of England, 1992, ISBN 1-853592-12-4. ★ (see also Videos)

Shennan S J (ed), **Archaeological Approaches to Cultural Identity**, Routledge, 1989, ISBN 0-04-445016-8.

Shettel, H, H et al, **Strategies for Determining Exhibit Effectiveness**, American Institutes for Research, 1968, Project V-011.

Shoard, M, **The Theft of the Countryside**, Temple Smith, 1980, ISBN 0-85117-201-6.

Stirling, A, **'Too Many Visitors?'** in ICOMOS Information, no.3, July/September 1990.

Stone, P G and Molyneaux B L (eds), **The Presented Past: Heritage, Museums and Education**, Routledge, 1994, ISBN 0-415-09602-2.

Stone, P G, **'The re-display of the Alexander Keiller Museum, Avebury, and the National Curriculum in England'** in The Presented Past, Stone, P G and Molyneaux, B L (eds), 1994, p 190-205.

Strike, J, **Architecture in Conservation: managing development at historic sites**, Routledge, 1994, ISBN 0-415-0830-0

Thompson, J M A, **The Manual of Curatorship**, Butterworth-Heinemann, 1984, ISBN 0-7506-0351-8.

Thompson, M W, **Ruins, their Preservation and Display**, British Museum Publications, 1981, ISBN 0-7141-8034-3.

Tilden, F, **Interpreting Our Heritage**, University of North Carolina Press, 1957, ISBN 0-8078-4016-5.

Tinniswood, A, **A History of Country House Visiting: Five Centuries of Tourism and Taste**, Blackwell, 1989, ISBN 0-631-14801-9.

Tittensor, R, **Conservation of our Historic Landscape Heritage**, FelphamPress, 1985, ISBN 0-870-69085-0.

Urban Planning and Regeneration, Hobsons/English Heritage/Commission for the New Towns, 1995, ISBN 1-86017-192-3. ★

Uzzell, D, **'The Hot Interpretation of War and Conflict in Heritage Interpretation**, Uzzell, D (ed), 1989a, p 33-47.

Uzzell, D (ed), **Heritage Interpretation: Vol 1 The Natural and Built Environment**, ISBN 1-85293-077-2; **Vol 2 The Visitor Experience**, ISBN 1-85293-078-0, Belhaven, 1989b.

Wagstaff, J M (ed), **Landscape and Culture: geographical and archaeological perspectives**, Blackwell, 1987, ISBN 0-631-15288-1

Waterson, M, **'Opening Doors on the Past'** in Heritage Interpretation, Uzzell, D (ed), 1989, p 48-56.

Woodbridge, K, **The Stourhead Landscape**, National Trust, 1989.

Wright, P, **On Living in an Old Country: The National Past in Contemporary Britain**, Verso, 1985, ISBN 0-86091-127-6.

EDUCATIONAL APPROACHES

Education on Site is a series of English Heritage teacher's guides which suggest educational strategies for using the historic environment as part of National Curriculum work.

Alderton, D, **Using industrial sites**, English Heritage, 1995. ISBN 1-85074-445-9. ★

Copeland, T, **Using castles**, English Heritage, 1993. ISBN 1-85074-327-4. ★

Copeland, T, **Geography and the historic environment**, English Heritage, 1993. ISBN 1-85074-332-0. ★

Copeland, T, **Maths and the historic environment**, English Heritage, 1992. ISBN 1-85074-329-0. ★

Durbin, G, **Using historic houses**, English Heritage, 1993. ISBN 1-85074-390-8. ★

Durbin, G, Morris, S & Wilkinson, S, **Learning from objects**, English Heritage, 1990.

ISBN 1-85074-259-6. ★
Keith, C, **Using listed buildings**, English Heritage, 1991. ISBN 1-85074-297-9. ★
Pownall, J & Hutson, **Science and the historic environment**, English Heritage, 1992. ISBN 1-85074-331-2. ★
Purkis, S, **Using memorials**, English Heritage, 1995. ISBN 1-85074-493-9. ★
Purkis, S, **Using school buildings**, English Heritage, 1993. ISBN 1-85074-379-7. ★
Wheatley, G, **World Heritage Sites**, English Heritage, forthcoming Autumn 1996. ISBN 1-85074-446-7.★

VIDEOS

Archaeology at Work introduces the methods and equipment used by archaeologists today.
Investigating towns, 1994, 30 minutes, English Heritage. How archaeologists recognise and record evidence in towns, using Liverpool and Shrewsbury as examples. ★
Looking for the past/Uncovering the past, 1994, 58 minutes, English Heritage. How archaeologists discover and record sites in the field and then the process of excavation at two rescue sites, one in the countryside and one in a town. ★

The Ferriby Boats - on the tides of time, 1994, 25 minutes, English Heritage. A documentary about the discovery and excavation of Bronze Age boats on the banks of the River Humber. ★
Framing Opinions - protecting our legacy of old windows, 1994, 26 minutes, English Heritage. Explains how the repair and upgrading of traditional windows can add to the historic and financial value of a property. ★
Making a point - pointing brickwork the traditional way, 1994, 30 minutes, English Heritage. Shows professionals how to use traditional, benign techniques and materials in repointing work. ★
A change of heart - English architecture since the war, 1992, 10 minutes, English Heritage. Illustrates the unsuspected wealth and range of fine architecture and design created in cities, towns and countryside since the Second World War. ★
The spirit of England, 1994, 60 minutes, Tadpole Lane/English Heritage. Guided tours to ten of the Historic Properties of English Heritage. ★
I am a tourist! Customer Service and Marketing, 1995, 29 minutes, English Heritage. A case study of Dover Castle for travel and tourism courses at post-16 level, especially GNVQ Travel and Tourism courses. ★
Changing Perceptions - Presenting Heritage, 1990, 26 minutes, University of Southampton. A case study of the presentation/interpretation of the World Heritage Site of Avebury. ★ Free loan only.

Frameworks of Worship is a series which examines the evidence, and the issues in church, cathedral and chapel studies. ★
Buildings and beliefs, 1990, 20 minutes, English Heritage. Demonstrates how the fabric of a parish church tells us about the social and religious beliefs of its builders. ★
Chapels - the buildings of non-conformity, 1989, 18 minutes, English Heritage. Investigates the varied forms, patterns and use of non-conformist building of worship. ★
God's Acre - nature conservation in the churchyard, 1993, 24 minutes, English Heritage. Shows good management practices and how a churchyard can be a focus of community worship. ★
In memoriam - the archaeology of graveyards, 1990, 21 minutes, English Heritage. Ecology, archaeology, art and social history may all be approached through the evidence which graveyards contain. ★
The master builders - the construction of a great church, 1991, 23 minutes, English Heritage. Explores the technology, engineering and design methods in the building of a cathedral, Beverley Minster. ★
Cathedral Archaeology, 1995, 21 minutes, English Heritage. Investigates the ways archaeologists record and excavate evidence in two cathedrals, Canterbury and Norwich, including the issues involved in working in a place of daily worship. ★

★ Indicates publications/videos which may be obtained from English Heritage postal sales - English Heritage, PO Box 229, Northampton NN6 9RY or ring 0171 973 3442 for a full catalogue.

Acknowledgements
We are extremely grateful for the help of colleagues at the School of Conservation Sciences, Bournemouth University for their advice and support and to Elizabeth McCrimmon for her assistance with the illustrations. Jo Jackson and family, Phillipa Hope and family, Cherry Trelogan and family, the Trustees of the Abbot Hall Art Gallery, Kendal. The editor would like to thank Fr. Distel of Gedenkstätte Dachau and the German Tourist Board for supplying the photograph of Dachau; Nick Brannon, Environment Service, Department of the Environment, Northern Ireland for finding the photographs which appear on page 9.

OPPOSITE: Listed telephone box in Elgin Avenue, Westminster, London. Red telephone boxes being replaced in the late 1980s by British Telecom caused controversy across the country as community groups and individuals fought campaigns to preserve them and, in some cases, have them protected by listing. This example is a K6 type designed in 1935. (English Heritage)

Our Education Service aims to help teachers at all levels make better use of the resource of the historic environment. Educational groups can make free visits to over 400 historic properties cared for by English Heritage. The following booklets are free on request. **Free Educational Visits**, **Using the Historic Environment**. Our **Resources** catalogue is also available. Please contact:

English Heritage Education Service 429 Oxford Street London W1R 2HD

Tel: 0171 973 3442 Fax: 0171 973 3443